RELIANT
THE FORGOTTEN FOUR-WHEELERS

MICHAEL BURGESS

AMBERLEY

First published 2025

Amberley Publishing
The Hill, Stroud,
Gloucestershire, GL5 4EP

www.amberley-books.com

ISBN: 978 1 3981 1423 4 (print)
ISBN: 978 1 3981 1424 1 (ebook)

British Library Cataloguing in Publication Data.
A catalogue record for this book is available from the British Library.

Typeset in 10pt on 13pt Celeste.
Typesetting by SJmagic DESIGN SERVICES, India.
Printed in the UK.

Appointed GPSR EU Representative: Easy Access System Europe Oü, 16879218
Address: Mustamäe tee 50, 10621, Tallinn, Estonia
Contact Details: gpsr.requests@easproject.com, +358 40 500 3575

Contents

Acknowledgements

The author and publisher would like to thank the following people/organisations for permission to use copyright material in this book: www.rs200.org for the image of the Ford RS200 rally car. CHG classics for images of the Reliant engine. Jim Pace for scans of the Anadol brochure. D & B auto spares, Chard, for access to their Ex-Haynes museum Metrocab. Cipher image courtesy of Steve Poole. Reliant Spares of Worcestershire for image of the Tempest kit car.

Every attempt has been made to seek permission for copyright material used in this book. However, if we have inadvertently used copyright material without permission/acknowledgement we apologise and we will make the necessary correction at the first opportunity.

Introduction

Today the sadly defunct Reliant marque is best remembered for their three-wheeled vehicles. Television's *Only Fools and Horses* made the yellow Regal Supervan a style icon, while comedian Jasper Carrot made a star of the phenomenally successful Reliant Robin (even if he would insist on referring to it as the Robin Reliant). Even Jeremy Clarkson felt the need to have a dig at them on *Top Gear*, repeatedly rolling his example and getting famous locals to help him push it upright. Later interviews had him admit that making the three-wheeled Reliant roll over was far harder than he had ever imagined. Welded-up back axles and massive amounts of carefully distributed extra weight were apparently involved.

Perennially popular in the industrial heartland of the UK where many of the working men were brought up riding motorcycles rather than driving cars, the three-wheeled Reliants could be driven on a motorcycle licence. Pre-1964 examples had to have no usable reverse gear (it was disabled but still present) to satisfy this condition, but soon just the light weight of the vehicle was sufficient to qualify. Their extensive use of the magic new lightweight material fibreglass saw to it that they always qualified on this score.

No matter how basic or outwardly crude looking, the enclosed Reliant three-wheeler was always warmer and drier than riding a motorcycle. The marque thrived despite competition from the manufacturers of other three-wheeled vehicles.

But there was much more to the products of the Reliant company than economy three-wheeled vehicles. They had contracts to produce fibreglass assemblies for other manufacturers, designed and produced ranges of vehicles for other countries and last but not least, behind the popular and famous three-wheeled vehicles there lurked a range of successful four-wheeled ones. It is to those neglected models this book is dedicated.

Where possible I have always quoted contemporary written sources of information such as road tests, sales brochures and press articles for my information. Given how versions of events can differ between people who were actually there, I hope readers will forgive me if the events related do not always exactly match their own memories.

1

The Company Background

The story of Reliant began in 1934 when Thomas Lawrence Williams purchased the rights to build a development of the three-wheeled Raleigh Safety Seven delivery van.

Legend has it that the first prototype was constructed in his garden at Kettlebrook near Tamworth in Staffordshire. This was a simple van powered by a 600 cc single-cylinder engine driving the rear axle via a chain. It was designed for small businesses to make local deliveries.

The first Reliant – a local delivery van derived from the Raleigh Safety Seven.

Williams had plans to develop the vehicle using the extra parts that had come with his purchase of the production rights. As many of these parts were already stamped with an 'R' for Raleigh, he worked his way through the 'R' section of the dictionary until he found a word that he felt suited the ethos of his planned new vehicle. The most suitable word he could find was Reliant, and a marque was born.

The van was available in both 7 cwt and 10 cwt forms, launched in 1935 and 1936 respectively. They were powered by proprietary JAP (standing for J. A. Prestwich industries) motorcycle engines.

Eager to increase their range, Reliant arranged from 1937 to use the four-cylinder 747 cc Austin Seven engine. When Austin ceased production of the engine in 1939 Reliant bought the rights to manufacture a version themselves and would develop it further.

Production continued until 1940 when war work took over. Production restarted in 1946 and the family of three-wheeled passenger vehicles for which Reliant will always be best known was launched in 1952 in the form of the three-wheeled Reliant Regal.

Initially utilising a body made of aluminium over a wooden fame, a huge step forwards was made in 1953 when some of the outer panels were produced in the new lightweight medium of moulded fibreglass.

Initially used as an insulation material, in 1936 Du Pont chemicals found a way of forming it into fixed shapes by mixing the raw fibres with a curing compound (an early version was called Cyanamid) to create strong, flexible sheets of a plastic-like material. By layering the material over a fixedmould, flexible but strong sections could be created. Once

Fibreglass – the miracle new material adopted by Reliant as early as 1953.

fixed to a more rigid sub-assembly such as a car chassis, the sections had considerable inherent strength.

The aviation industry was an early adopter of this lightweight material, as were builders who could suddenly get light, cheap preformed sections of guttering and the like. By the 1950s it was being looked at by small-volume car manufacturers as a lighter, cheaper alternative to conventional metal bodies. With a gel-coat applied over the top of the rough fibres it could be painted to produce results visually indistinguishable from those of a metal-bodied car.

By 1956 the entire external body was made from fibreglass and the Reliant's association with the material was firmly founded. A 1966 press release would describe Reliant as Europe's largest manufacturer of glass-fibre-bodied cars and commercial vehicles. Many consider they were the largest users in the world, especially when their production of other parts and products not motoring related were included. Unlike metal which required considerable skill to construct into a car body, creating one in fibreglass from a mould required far less training.

Reliant were not, however, the first motoring manufacturer to see the advantages of the new lightweight medium. Berkley cars of Biggleswade in Bedfordshire would be the first to give their cars a fibreglass body, beating Reliant to that claim by a matter of weeks. A tiny three-wheeled vehicle with the two wheels at the front rather than at the rear, as was the case of the Reliant Regal, it was an open sporting design aimed at a very different market.

To create a fibreglass car body a basic mould was created from a full-sized styling buck of the finished vehicle and the various shaped layers of the fibreglass matting were laid

The first production car manufactured from fibreglass, the Berkley sports car.

into the mould by hand. Images of the time show workers cutting the sections of medically irritating matting to shape by hand with no protection such as masks or gloves. How times have changed.

A smooth external gel-coat was applied to the mould first by spray and allowed to dry before being followed by several layers of pre-cut fibres soaked in a two-part catalyst resin that bonded them all together to produce a light, strong body. Once cured the result was a strong, flexible structure considerably lighter and easier to construct than the same structure in sheet steel.

At the height of production the Reliant bodyshop, with their experienced and reportedly enthusiastic staff, could produce thirty-five complete vehicle bodies during an eight-hour shift.

As production increased Reliant outgrew their premises regularly and would eventually occupy a sprawling site at Two Gates in Tamworth, Shropshire. The A5 main road split the site as much of the space they occupied had been purchased as it became available around their original premises. When the demands for space on the original site became too great further sites were purchased at Shenstone and Kettlebrook.

The 13-acre Shenstone factory was once home to the Alliance stamping factory and was some 7 miles away from the original Two Gates site. It was opened by World Champion racing driver Jim Clark in November 1963 driving a Reliant three-wheeler through a ribbon across the main gates.

The aim at Reliant was for engine and large mechanical assembly production to be centralised at the new Shenstone factory. At the height of production, around 400 of their own engines were being produced per week, along with gearboxes to fit them.

Kettlebrook was acquired in 1965 following a fire at the Two Gates factory. A mile away from the factory site, it would eventually become the home of the Reliant body production line. Reliant produced their own custom-weight fibreglass matting in-house in three weights depending on the load-bearing requirements of different parts of the bodyshell, then cut the mat to the pattern shapes required to be bonded together to form the bodies.

When the Regal 3/25 arrived in 1962 a landmark was reached when Reliant finally did away with the wooden bracing under the body and created one of the world's first fibreglass monocoque construction cars. (The Lotus Elite would claim to be the first, launched in 1957.) This process made the panels stressed sections that supported each other and created a rigid assembly. The windscreen was also a stressed part of the body structure to keep the body from flexing.

The body was constructed of two large sections (inner and outer), which were bonded together on a jig then bolted to the metal chassis as a single unit. This was a process Reliant would to use for nearly all their vehicles from here on.

By the late 1960s Reliant dominated the three-wheeled car market in the UK, and arguably the world.

Reliant had two main competitors in their field of fibreglass three-wheeled economy vehicles and sporting executive saloons: Bond cars at Preston in Lancashire (of whom more later) and Gilbern cars near Pontypridd in South Wales. Likewise powered by the Ford Essex V6 engine used in the Reliant Scimitar, the Gilbern range kept prices down by offering their vehicles as partially completed kits of parts that the purchaser completed in their home garages to avoid the imposition of purchase tax. The imposition of VAT

This 1966 brochure proudly boasts Reliant was Europe's largest manufacturer of fibreglass vehicles. Many would suggest 'in the world' was more accurate.

on all vehicles from 1973 was the death knell to Gilbern and the Reliant Scimitar had the executive fibreglass car market to itself.

For many years Reliant had also produced fibreglass cabs and seven-seat crew-cab units for Ford D series trucks and later hi-tops for their Ford Transit and Escort vans. The crew cabs would go on to be developed for other Ford products, Merryweather fire engines and eventually be developed with a new nose section for the Chrysler Commando commercial vehicle range.

This product had started life as a venture to produce fibreglass cabs for Ford 'D' series trucks in overseas factories where the price of steel was prohibitive and local skills lacking. Reliant designed an innovative double-skinned cab that was easy to build for relatively unskilled fabricators that offered far greater refinement than other single-skinned cabs that Ford had been experimenting with.

Above: Reliant produced cabs for the Ford D series lorry for many years, this press photo being of the 100th example photographed on 2 June 1966.

Right: The Ford D series cab production line.

Reliant would also make a name for themselves producing complete fibreglass bodyshells for other manufacturers. During the 1980s Reliant provided the bodies and assembled the limited production homologation special Ford RS200 (so named as 200 examples had to be produced for competition homologation purposes) rally car.

Plans to build a revised version of the SAAB Sonnet sports coupé at Reliant in fibreglass got as far as design mock-ups and styling sketches before the plans fell through.

Reliant also turned their expertise in fibreglass to creating a range of non-motoring products, including nose cones for railway engines and covers for air-conditioning units.

One of their stranger projects was the Skooter Ski water scooter. A forerunner of what would today be called a Jet Ski, the Scooter Ski was powered by a Rotax single-cylinder engine.

Designed by Tim Bedford, who had no production facilities for his new design, he turned to Reliant for their famed experience in the field of fibreglass production. The first order was for 2,500 units, quickly followed by another 1,000 following the 1970 Boat Show. Making the best of the publicity available with the new product, press photographs were produced showing the Skooter Ski being towed on a trailer behind a Reliant Scimitar coupé.

Competition in the fast-growing market of small recreational water craft brought production to an end by the middle of the 1970s.

For the bulk of their life the Reliant motor company would remain synonymous with the use of fibreglass in their many products, motoring and otherwise.

Reliant's last production contract with Ford was to produce the bodies for and to assemble 200 homologation special RS200 rally cars. (Photo courtesy of www.rs200.org)

Above: Reliant will always be best known for their range of three-wheeled niche market vehicles. Their most famous, the Robin, is shown here.

Below: Always keen to publicise their products, here we see one of theirs promoted as the mount of television's 'Scribblemobile'.

2

Sabra, Sabre, and the Israeli Connection

The story of the Reliant Sabre that would give birth to their best-known four-wheeled car, the Reliant Scimitar, had unusual beginnings in what was then the new country of Israel.

The national car maker of Israel was Autocars Limited, established by the Israeli government at Haifa. They were established to produce cars for local consumption from fibreglass. Initially they produced the three-wheeled Regent, but as three-wheeled vehicles did not enjoy any favourable tax or driving licence rules in Israel, Reliant were approached to produce a four-wheeled version.

The Sussita was an amalgam of the rear of the three-wheeled Reliant Regal, a simple front end enclosed in a basic fibreglass body.

A specification was issued that the new four-wheeled vehicle should be able to carry a 10-cwt load at 50 miles per hour over the rough Israeli roads. There should also be scope for later body versions to be developed on the same chassis as commercials and pick-up trucks.

Reliant developed a four-wheeled van version of their three-wheeled Regal called the Regent Four, which was sent to Israel in kit form for local assembly. This was followed by the Sussita (Horse in Hebrew) launched in 1960. It mated the rear of the three-wheeled Reliant Regal with a unique front end to create a four-wheeled vehicle that would be produced from 1962 to 1964.

The rear of the chassis was very similar to the established three-wheeled range while the front had coil-sprung independent suspension to cope with the poor local road conditions.

It was designed by Reliant to provide basic transportation and was available as a two-door saloon or pick-up truck. Like UK Reliants the bodyshell was made of fibreglass mounted on a sturdy chassis. Being larger than the UK models of the time, Reliant's own engine was considered insufficiently powerful, so the Ford Popular 34 horsepower side valve engine was used, driving the rear wheels through a Ford Popular three-speed gearbox. 1962 would see the engine and gearbox upgraded to the overhead valve unit from the new Ford Anglia. Reliant would supply over 6,000 kits of parts over the next five years.

Autocars would export Sussitas to America (admittedly in tiny numbers), as well as a number of other countries. A handful were retained and registered for use in the UK by Reliant themselves as service vans.

The Sussita, seen front on, shows the 'parts bin' origins of many of the parts.

The estate car version of the Sussita offered basic family transport to the Israeli market.

The Sussita would be joined by a family saloon called Carmel, vehicles (named after a mountain that overlooked Haifa) also assembled from CKD (complete knocked down) kits from Reliant.

This again featured a rear very similar to the Reliant Regal with a reverse sloped rear window common to the newly launched Ford Anglia, a vehicle from which it took its engine and gearbox.

Again as a nod to the poor road conditions it was expected to encounter in Israel the suspension system was unexpectedly advanced, with a Triumph-derived swing axle of the rear and full independent suspension on the front with coil springs and dampers.

Both Sussita and Carmel were restyled for 1964 and the briefly fashionable reverse sloped rear window was replaced by a more conventional-looking design.

Legend has it that the head of Autocars, Yitzhak Shubinsky, was browsing the UK racing car show in 1960 looking for designs that he could turn into a new sporting design for the Israeli market. Impressed by both a new chassis design by Leslie Bellamy and the fibreglass-bodied Ashley 1172 special, he purchased the rights to use both as a starting point for his new design. The Ashley fibreglass body was designed to fit on the existing Ford Popular chassis to create a more sporting-looking vehicle cheaply when the original metal bodyshell began to rust away. The Ashley fibreglass fabrication company still lives on today, producing fibreglass coupé conversions and flip-up front ends for classic cars.

He then walked across the show hall to the Reliant stand and commissioned them to put them together and modify both to create his new sporting car. The original plan was that Reliant would supply kits of mechanical parts and the moulds to allow Autocars to manufacture the bodies themselves.

The production line with the estate version seen front left and Sabra convertibles in the background.

Never one to shirk a challenge, and no doubt thankful that both designs were of very similar proportions, Reliant took only nine months to develop a design that made use of the best parts of both designs and replaced the original side valve engine with a new 1700 cc Ford Consul 375 unit, largely as it would easily fit in the space available under the bonnet line of the Ashley bodyshell. This massively improved performance over the Ashley prototype. The Ford engine produced 72 horsepower against the originally installed side valve engine's output of 34 horsepower.

Joining the two disparate parts led to much innovation and cunning at Reliant. The body moulds provided by Ashley were designed to bolt onto an existing Ford chassis, so lacked a floor. To avoid the cost and time implications of creating completely new moulds in the Reliant style they chose to adopt floor boards made of marine-grade plywood bonded into place (not uncommon at the time), and to make everything fit together, the parts bins of many manufacturers were raided. Reliant's own three-wheeled Regent van supplied the rear coil springs and axle, and the little-known Meadows Frisky microcar gave up its windscreen. Given the sporting nature of the vehicle, Reliant did not adopt their usual four-speed gearbox from Ford but installed a sportier close ratio but more expensive unit produced by German manufacturer ZF. Many of the road tests of the time commented favourably on the short gear lever movement and all gear synchromesh of this unit, usually only seen in far more expensive vehicles such as the Lotus Elite.

Like the Triumph Herald/Spitfire range, the whole nose cone of the Sabra Sport tipped forward to give easy access to the engine. To suit the intended American market the nose had two large chromed overriders moulded permanently in place to protect the bodywork form parking incidents.

Inside the Sabra displayed a well-equipped dashboard with two big-hooded binnacles in front of the driver housing a rev counter and speedometer flanking a clock, and four ancillary gauges displayed beneath.

Happy with the result, Yitzhak Shubinsky christened it Sabra Sport (the Sussita range had been marketed in the USA under the same brand, the word meaning born in Israel, and also a genus of cactus) and thought it the ideal car to export to the United States. Sold in the United States alongside the Sussita and the Carmel, the Sabra Sport was available in ST (soft top) and HT (hard top) forms.

A poster advert for the newly anglicised Reliant Sabre advertising the launch at stand 146 of the Motor Show.

He commissioned Reliant to produce the first 208 examples, with around 140 being exported directly to America following the Sabra's debut at the 1961 New York World's Fair. The example on the stand was mechanically incomplete, but the Sabra Sport still received a favourable reception. The balance of that first batch of Reliant-built cars made their way into various markets within Europe. Despite their UK origins for political and tax reasons their production plates clearly stated they were the product of Autocars Ltd Haifa Israel.

Following this export order, Reliant produced around fifty Sabras as CKD kits, which were sent direct to Israel for local assembly before being re-exported to their destination countries, of which Belgium was their largest market.

Autocars of Israel would enter receivership in 1971, although by this time most of their ties with Reliant had been ended following Shubinsky signing what he hoped would be a more beneficial deal with UK-based British Leyland.

Seeing the resulting American interest in the Sabra, Reliant considered production for the UK market. They converted a prototype to right-hand drive and, while retaining the same basic engine, they offered two engine tuning packages from well-known tuning company Alexander Engineering of Haddenham, Buckinghamshire. Stage two (the car was viewed as being in a 'stage one' state of tune in standard form) would offer an increased

The front of the first Sabre sales brochure clearly showing the divisive styling of the 'boomerang' front bumper overriders.

compression ratio while retaining a single Solex carburettor producing 110 horsepower. Stage three would add a modified cylinder head and twin SU carburettors and produce around 130 horsepower. The first gave a modest increase in performance while the latter turned the Sabra into a genuine 100 miles per hour car. The less tuned engines offered top speeds of between 80 and 90 miles per hour while the 0–60 time for the 'standard' engine was listed as 15.4 seconds.

Autocar magazine would record a 0–60 time of 16.6 seconds and a top speed of 90 miles per hour. Fuel consumption was considered reasonable at 28 miles per gallon.

In the interests of making the car sound more British, the Sabra name was amended to Sabre, a type of sword with a hand guard and a curved blade intended for cavalry use. Internally, it would be known as the SE1.

The Reliant Sabre was launched on the UK market in 1961 at the Earls Court Motor Show. It represented Reliant's first move into the mainstream four-wheeled market and their first sports model. It received a very mixed reception.

The very prominent 'L' (some sources described them as boomerang shaped) bumper overriders either side of the mesh radiator grille were retained for cost reasons and were not to the taste of every journalist.

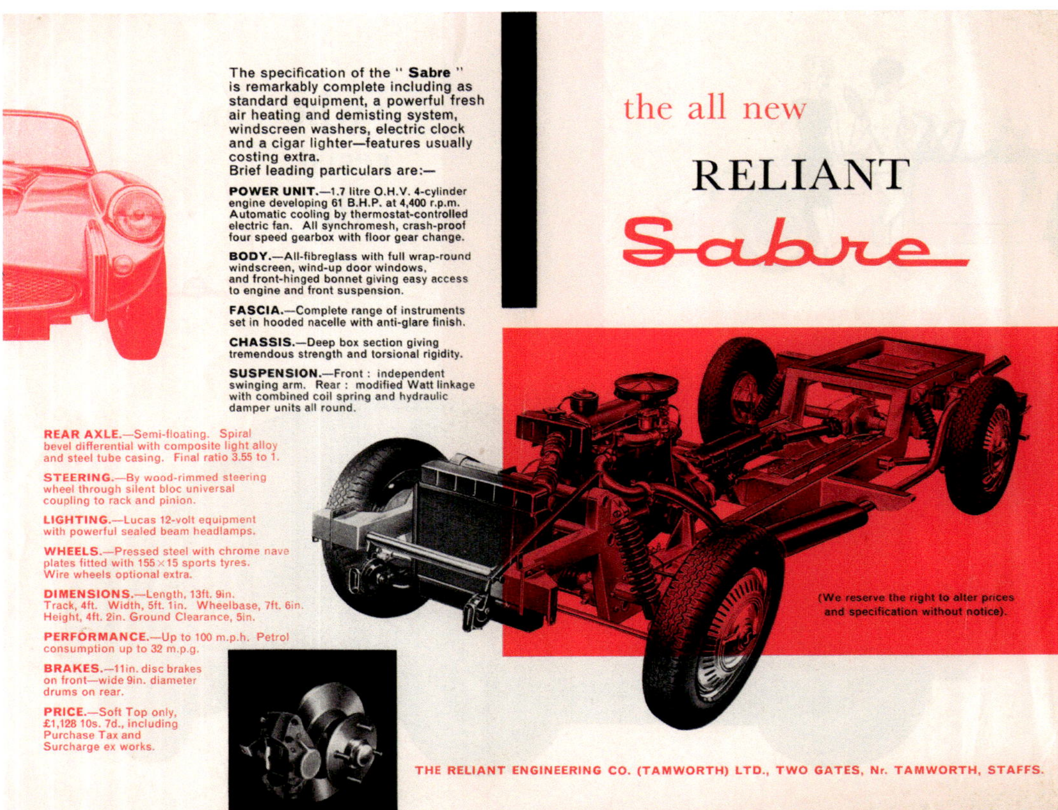

The rear of the Sabre brochure showed an image of the bare chassis beneath the stylish body.

Others had misgivings about the idiosyncratic independent front suspension and tip-forwards bonnet, even though in practice both systems worked very well.

Part of the licensing deal for the chassis had included the stipulation that the suspension mounting points could not be changed and a quantity of parts had been included in the deal, so the unusual leading arm suspension was retained. Later writers would unkindly refer to it as 'flappy arm' front suspension.

The original chassis had featured transverse mounted leaf springs both front and rear. Reliant had replaced the front transverse spring with coil over damper units for production to enable the lower nose of the Ashley body to accommodate the new Ford engine they had chosen.

At the rear of the Sabre the live axle was located by coil spring damper units produced by famous British company Girling, all located by an unusual arrangement of suspension arms. Those at the bottom of the suspension faced forwards while those at the top faced rearwards. Girling would also provide the breaking system, with discs at the front and drums at the rear.

There were occasional comments that the ride was rough (the system only offered a suspension travel of 5 inches) but many journalists expected nothing less and labelled the ride 'sporting'.

For October 1961 the Sabre was updated. The earlier version with the Ford Consul 375 engine became retrospectively known as the Sabre Four, and the new version the Sabre Six, internally known as the SE2.

The four-cylinder Consul 375 engine was replaced after some debate with the Ford six-cylinder 2.5-litre engine from the Zephyr/Zodiac range. This was a basic but extremely sturdy engine with the crankshaft running on four main bearings and produced 109 horsepower in standard form. This gave the new Sabre Six a top speed of 110 miles per hour and a 0–60 time of 12.2 seconds. A touring miles per gallon figure of around

Seen here in an official publicity photo, the facelifted Sabre Six saw the nose completely redesigned.

30 miles per gallon was considered normal for a performance car of the type, while a more active driver might, according to road tests of the time, manage in the low twenties.

Press captions from the time describe the Sabre Six as 'provides luxury 120 m.p.h. motoring for a basic price of less than £850', while some press pictures listed a starting price of £890.

In the interest of keeping prices low and the paperwork of using multiple suppliers down, the new six-cylinder engine was mated to a Ford Zodiac gearbox that still offered synchromesh on all forward gears instead of the more expensive German ZF gearbox.

The front suspension was revised to a double wishbone and coil system that was common to the current Triumph TR series sports cars after the first fifteen Sabre Sixes were supplied with the older Sabre Four system, which was itself carried over from the use of Ford transverse mounted leaf springs and swing axles used on the original Leslie Bellamy-designed chassis.

The controversial front styling was addressed by the removal of the oft-commented-upon overriders and a more conventional-looking full-width bumper fitted.

The front styling now had a squared-off look rather than the longer and rounded nose of the original. The earlier pronounced nose overhang was sharply reduced, shortening the length of the Sabra Six by 7 inches. The grille was restyled into two separate square sections with wire inserts with a vertical column in the centre. The earlier round front lights were replaced by compound and widely used Lucas square types that incorporated side lights and indicators in the same unit. The chrome-trimmed bonnet scoop from the

These official publicity images of the Sabre Six convertible were widely circulated but the vehicle never reached volume production.

Sabra sourced from the Austin Westminster was also deleted, the bonnet now featuring an enclosed bulge to clear the engine beneath.

The rear wheel arches were remoulded to a more rounded profile, the coupé roof gaining an air extractor scoop moulded into the roof to allow ventilation for the occupants. The Austin A40 Farina would supply new, neater rear lights and be a rare departure from parts gathered from the Ford parts bin.

Curiously there was no boot as such on the Reliant Sabre Six, only a horizontal compartment which housed the spare wheel and the tools needed to change it.

Steel wheels were supplied as standard, but many owners opted for the optional wire wheels. All came shod with the famous Pirelli Cinturato tyres.

For reasons unknown there was never an open version of the Sabre Six, although enthusiastic later owners would create some of their own. Two prototypes were displayed on the Reliant stand at the 1962 Earls Court Motor Show but it never reached full production. As proper publicity photographs were produced with typed captions on them describing the convertible as being 'in production form', we can only speculate as to why production at Reliant did not go ahead.

Despite the updates and favourable reviews (*Autocar* magazine considered the Sabre Six 'a fine touring car' and prised both the driver visibility and driving position) the Sabre Six was not a sales success.

Reliant entered into a rally competition programme that remains most famous for a spectacular crash on the 1964 Monte Carlo Rally where the works Sabre Six suffered a

Seen from the rear, this Sabre Six convertible displays the carefully packaged hood storage and the comprehensively equipped dashboard.

puncture at speed on a road with no walls. The Sabra Six rolled some 80 feet down a rocky slope to end up battered at the bottom. Both drivers walked away from the wreck unhurt, which was a stunning testament to the strength of the standard bodyshell but brought their rally to an end.

Reliant advertising would, however, trumpet their first and second places in the 2.5-litre GT category in the Alpine Rally. Sadly the true potential of the Sabre as a competition car only really came to the fore in private hands, and even more so as a choice driving in classic car rallies.

These competition programmes brought them publicity but sadly no sales and production of the Sabre Six ended in 1964. Seventy-five GTs and the two convertibles were produced. Plans to create a V8-engined version of the Sabre using the Rover 3.5-litre V8 engine, which would have been known as an SE3, sadly never reached production, but explained why the next four-wheeled car Reliant produced would be known as the SE4.

3

The Reliant Engine

Reliant were always keen to make as much of their products in-house as they could, and one area in which their small cars were unique was in their choice of engine.

All Reliant's competitors in the three-wheeled markets used proprietary engines bought in from outside manufacturers. Their closest competitors at manufacturer Bond in Preston, Lancashire, powered their three-wheeled Minicars with motorcycle engines by Villiers, and much later with a detuned version of the Hillman Imp engine.

The Reliant philosophy of producing as much of their vehicles in-house most unusually extended to the engines.

After a brief flirtation with JAP motorcycle engines, Reliant vehicles were powered by the Austin four-cylinder engine as used in the Austin Seven. When Austin ceased production of this engine Reliant purchased the production rights and tooling to continue the manufacture for their own use with a few amendments to suit their smaller-scale manufacturing needs.

The position of the distributer was changed and a number of vital dimensions were amended, which enabled Reliant to both improve the now elderly engine design and to ensure that owners had to buy their spares from Reliant and not from local Austin dealerships. The new engine design was first run on 3 September 1939, producing 14.5 horsepower.

In 1959 Reliant considered it time to design a new, more advanced four-cylinder engine for their vehicles.

They found themselves in possession of a Chinese copy of a cast-iron Standard Motor Company four-cylinder engine. Chief engineer Ron Heathcoate set about recreating and refining this design into their own unique overhead valve engine. Among their aims was a considerable drop in weight, greater reliability and lower servicing requirements.

When the early prototypes proved between 50 and 60 pounds heavier than the old 747 cc side valve engines, they took the bold step of recasting the engine in aluminium to create an engine over 20 kg lighter than the original.

Birmingham aluminium specialists Birmal were consulted and considerable investment was involved, but soon Reliant could legitimately claim to be the producers of the UK's first mass-produced aluminium engine. They would beat the Rootes group Hillman Imp family to this title by a matter of weeks.

Above left: The first Reliant engine in its original location, the Austin Seven 747 cc engine.

Above right: The inlet and exhaust side of the yellow-top Reliant alloy engine. (Photo courtesy of CHG classics)

Like most aluminium engines of this era, the pistons of the Reliant engine ran in steel cylinder bore liners made of high tensile centrifugally cast iron to ensure strength and longevity for the engine.

A massive test and development programme was set in place where staff members were given three-wheeled Reliant Regals to use with the aim of each one covering at least 100,000 miles under all conditions before the engines were returned to the workshops to be stripped and checked for unusual wear. Considerable high-speed motorway use was claimed by the factory at the time in those days of no 70-mph speed limit. On inspection a remarkable lack of wear was encountered and the engine was considered ready for mass production.

Using a single Solex carburettor, the new engine produced 24.2 horsepower from a capacity of 600 cc where the fully developed 747 cc iron engine had only produced 17.5 horsepower.

First seeing service in the three-wheeled Regal Supervan, the new 600 cc engine was both more efficient and lighter than its predecessor; it could offer the vehicle the same performance as with the earlier 747 cc engine.

Popular rumours persist that such was the demand for the new aluminium engine and the size of stock still held of the now redundant side valve unit that large numbers were buried under the site of the old woodworking shop until recently used to create the wood framing for Regals as part of the foundations for the new buildings.

Following comments on contemporary road tests and comments from drivers of the heavier Reliant Rebel, 1968 would see the capacity of the Reliant engine increased to 700 cc. With the adoption of the superior Zenith carburettor power output was raised to 31.5 horsepower (the three-wheeled Regal would receive a less powerful 29 horsepower version).

By 1969 *Motor* magazine claimed Reliant had already produced 110,000 examples of their engine.

A 750 cc development arrived in 1972 alongside a new gearbox. First trialled in the Rebel, this version would find its way into the phenomenally successful Robin three-wheeled range in 1973. Power output rose to 32 horsepower alongside a noticeable increase in torque to create a more relaxing and refined driving experience.

For 1975 the Reliant engine would see the last increase in capacity to 850 cc. Finally adopting the variable choke SU carburettor used by most of the UK car industry, power output would rise to 40 horsepower, which offered all of Reliant's small cars a respectable turn of speed alongside the competition.

The distributer side of the yellow-top Reliant engine. Earlier examples would feature a red top. (Picture courtesy of CHG classics)

The 850 cc version of the Reliant engine would become the most numerous incarnation of the engine, with production continuing until the entire Reliant small car range ceased production in 2002.

Experiments to produce a higher torque and greater economy from the engine in 1984 known as the HTE version (High Torque Economy, visually identified by a yellow colour rocker cover rather than the normal red one) were not a success. By changing compression ratios and camshaft profile, torque was increased by more than 7 per cent, which allowed for a higher axle ratio for increased refinement and a more relaxing driving experience at the expense of ultimate power output.

The introduction of unleaded petrol in the UK led to complaints of heavy engine knocking under load ('pinking' to use the colloquial term). Reliant issued a press release clearly stating that the new unleaded petrol should not be used with the HTE engine but problems persisted, so the engine specification was returned to the older 40 horsepower system, which would remain until production of the engine ceased.

Racing engines manufacturers BRM were involved in potential further developments of the 850 cc version of the Reliant engine. They developed a twin overhead camshaft cylinder head for the engine that would mount twin SU carburettors to raise the output to around 70 horsepower, and experimented with modern fuel injection systems. Running prototypes were produced but the engine never reached production.

In common with most alloy engines of this era, the pistons ran in steel sleeves within the alloy bores. Seen here on a non-Reliant engine as an example.

4

Rebel

The early three-wheeled Reliants started life as aluminium bodies over a wooden frame atop a conventional steel chassis. Slowly but surely the weight and complexity of these vehicles was reduced through the use of the then new material fibreglass.

The 'specials boom' of the 1950s saw many small companies springing up to supply lightweight fibreglass bodies designed to be bolted straight onto the chassis of old vehicles to give them a new look. Basic and staid upright saloons from the 1930s could be transformed (at least as far as their styling was concerned) into more modern or sporting-looking machines.

Many of the bodies were hand finished and were of what might be described as 'indeterminate' quality and depended entirely on the skill of the builder to create a good-looking vehicle as a result.

At Reliant, with their fast-growing market for three-wheeled vehicles, long-standing company managing director Ray Wiggin looked at people's increasing desire to own four-wheeled vehicles if they could and planned a small four-wheeled car for Reliant. He believed that the loyal purchasers of three-wheeled Reliant products which could then be driven on a motorcycle licence would buy a small four-wheeled car if they produced one once they passed their full driving test. He also believed that once the post-war hard times started to fade, the fad for three-wheeled vehicles might pass and that Reliant should make plans for this future. The result of this plan became the small saloon named the Reliant Rebel.

Their regular stylist Tom Karen at Ogle design was commissioned to design a body for a chassis similar to those used in the three-wheeled cars, which was designed in-house by engineer David Page and his team. One of the main requirements were that the design should use as many current Reliant mechanical parts as possible while still being light and more rigid than the three-wheeled cars and having a unique look.

Tom Karen was an interesting character famous for his designs in many fields after he took over Ogle design following the death of company founder David Ogle in 1962. Born in Vienna, he was raised in Czechoslovakia. Fleeing the advancing Nazis in 1939, he and his family ended up, like many of his countrymen, in England.

The Reliant Rebel, the clean line of the body gives a "perky" appearance and a distinctive line.
NO FEE FOR REPRODUCTION PRESS ENQUIRIES: Peter R. Orton, LUDgate Circus 7200

Above: The official description of the styling of the Rebel as being 'perky' appears in this press photo, as well as showing the early double-height radiator grille.

Below: The estate version of the Rebel had a 7-inch longer, taller and squarer rear body shape for load access and space.

RELIANT REBEL 700 ESTATE - glass fibre, 700 c.c., four cylinders, 70 m.p.h., four seater

He remains most famous for his extensive design work for Reliant, although his other design masterpiece, the Raleigh Chopper children's bicycle, is equally fondly remembered by a whole generation. Other motoring projects included the interior of the Ford 105E Anglia and he won awards for his design work for Hotpoint washing machines.

The rear of the Reliant Rebel chassis not unsurprisingly echoed the basic ladder construction of the three-wheeled Reliant Regal, with a section added to the front to support the extra wheel. The steering and front suspension were courtesy of a Burman Douglas-type steering box from the Standard Ten saloon linked to front suspension uprights, wishbones and trunions of the Triumph Herald. This equipped the Rebel with the same remarkably small 27-foot turning circle as the donor Herald. The Tom Karen body design was especially space efficient, offering excellent interior space for the size of vehicle (a skill apparently now sadly lost to the motoring world) as the engine could be moved considerably further forward than in the three-wheeled vehicles.

Fashioned from fibreglass, it was also very light and fitted with a 24 horsepower 600 cc version of the in-house Reliant engine, which offered a claimed 60 miles per gallon economy while easily achieving 60 miles per hour top speed (66 was the actual quoted figure).

Sadly the general performance and refinement lagged behind the more mass-produced and better-developed vehicles of the opposition. There was, for instance, no synchromesh on first gear, and later cars were still criticised in road tests for poor gear selection and synchromesh right up until the end of production.

The 1966 Rebel saloon boasted an improved and uprated interior.

Being a rather more handmade product, it was more expensive that the mass-produced competition, but Ray Wiggin was correct in thinking that Reliant owners would remain loyal to the brand and the Rebel sold in small but steady numbers.

The Reliant Rebel saloon was launched at the Earls Court Motor Show in 1964 alongside the new Scimitar GT coupé. Road tests spoke of excellent handling and road holding, but the words 'Utilitarian' and 'underpowered' were used more than once (the benchmark 0–60 time took a whole 36 seconds, which was considered slow even by 1964 standards). Reliant chose to make much of the rust-free fibreglass body feature by using the advertising slogan 'No need for a garage'.

A revised Rebel arrived in 1965 with improved rear suspension and an updated interior. The underpowered engine was uprated to 27 horsepower, giving a much-needed boost to performance. The economy remained excellent and a much-voiced selling point, the adverts still claiming 60 miles per hour and 60 miles per gallon.

RELIANT REBEL 700 ESTATE - two-door, four/five seater in glass fibre.

The Rebel estate introduced what would become the small Reliant estate trademark of the side hinged rear door.

RELIANT REBEL 700 - glass fibre, 700 c.c., 70 m.p.h., 60 m.p.g., four seater family saloon

This official publicity photo clearly shows the different shape of the rear body on the Rebel saloon.

In an attempt to answer these issues a further updated version of the Rebel arrived in October 1967 in the form of the Rebel 700. The 600 cc version of the Reliant engine was replaced with the latest 700 cc version fitted with a Zenith carburettor. This new engine produced 31 horsepower along with a useful 17 per cent rise in torque at a low 2500 rpm, which made the engine far more flexible, making driving the Rebel a far more pleasant experience. These improvements could push the Rebel to 68 miles per hour according to the launch press release while still retaining a very respectable 55 miles per gallon (road tests found around 45 miles per gallon was more likely). Not quite as eye-catching in the advertising stakes, but a very noticeable improvement.

Sadly, even with the useful increase in power output the 0–60 miles per hour time was quoted as an incredibly slow 31.5 seconds. Actual road tests would manage 72 miles per hour and a 0–60 time of 30.2 seconds.

Inside the Rebel was updated again to try and close the perceived gap between Reliant and their mainstream competitors. There was a new padded dashboard with two instrument clusters and, for the first time, a multi-function steering column switch. The heater remained listed as an optional extra. At launch the Rebel 700 was listed as being available in rebel red, golden brown, Aztec blue, honey beige, greenstone and sunburst yellow.

The revised interior of the Rebel offered a faux walnut dash panel and a wrap-over instrument cluster that would live on in other small Reliants for many years.

Alongside the Rebel saloon, Reliant launched the Rebel estate. With a body 7 inches longer than the saloon, it offered a useful increase in carrying capacity and a higher, straight roofline. Adverts spoke of 46 cubic feet of interior space with the seats folded or 20 cubic feet with the seats raised. To make the best of this longer body the chassis was modified to allow a wider, flatter load-carrying area by relocating the petrol tank.

The estate would be the first small Reliant to feature what would become their signature small estate car rear design of a single large door opening to the side. It would be seen again on the 1973 Robin and other small Reliants that came after it.

Above: Seen side on, the Rebel estate/van offered a superbly ergonomic design to offer the finest accommodation the 7-inch-longer body could offer.

Left: To allow easy access to the load space the rear door of the estate/van takes up the whole of the rear of the body, leaving no edges to lift loads over.

The estate soon became the best-selling member of the Rebel range, something that would be echoed elsewhere in the Reliant range in the form of the Scimitar GTE over the coupé.

Overseas sales were achieved in such exotic markets as Angola and Bermuda, followed by more mainstream European markets such as Portugal.

Motor magazine would road test the Rebel in 700 cc estate form in 1971 and found it capable of 70 miles per hour while returning 50 miles per gallon. The 0–60 miles per hour sprint was covered in 33.1 seconds.

They considered the Rebel's economy second only to the FIAT 500 Giardinitra. The lack (still) of synchromesh on first gear and slightly unusual gear ratios attracted comment and they found the ride rough. They considered the handling good and according to them an Austin Healey Sprite (a small, current but also rather dated sports car design) had to be driven hard to keep up with their test car, which speaks highly of the handling.

In October 1972 Reliant produced their final update to the Rebel. The header of the press release claimed a 'smoother more powerful engine, challenges small foreign cars'. The latest 750 cc version of the Reliant engine was fitted, along with an interior update that was shared with the three-wheeled range and the latest Scimitars. There was a strip of fake woodwork on the dashboard alongside a new instrument unit that wrapped around the steering wheel.

The interior of the Rebel was well appointed and the seats comfortable. (Non-standard automatic seen here, created by this car's owner.)

There was also a new range of colours to make what was now a dated-looking design stand out in the showrooms. Synchromesh would finally reach all the forwards gears in 1972, just in time for the launch of the new Reliant Robin, and would add a smooth hydraulic clutch to the package.

A van version was also introduced to appeal to small businesses, which was effectively the Rebel estate without side windows or rear seats. The Post Office was specifically targeted as a customer as they were seeking a replacement for their Morris Minor van fleet at the time. They took ten vehicles on trial but sadly for Reliant the huge fleet order never materialised.

The Rebel van was an easy extra model to produce and it took less labour to manufacture the body as the panels for windows did not need to be cut out prior to trimming. Supplied only in primer so any business could add their own colour scheme, it sold poorly but remained listed until Rebel production ended. Devious owners could order a van, pay less tax as it was a commercial vehicle and purchase a side window kit from the supplying dealer to convert it to a saloon themselves.

This latest version of the well-proven Reliant engine produced 35 horsepower, which produced reasonable performance in the lightweight Rebel. The top speed was now 75 miles per hour (early press releases spoke of 'around seventy miles per hour') while economy rose to a heady 63 miles per gallon at a steady 30 miles per hour and 48 miles per gallon at a steady 50 miles per hour according to Reliant's own press release. They said the Rebel could make a 'fair claim' to be the most economical four-wheeled car available on the British market. The inevitable 0–60 figure sat at 23.2 seconds.

Production of the Reliant Rebel ended in 1974, shortly after the incredibly successful Reliant Robin was launched in 1973. Sales were in serious decline by then, the Rebel both looking and feeling dated and Reliant desperately needing the production capacity the Rebel was taking up for the Robin range.

Around 3,500 Reliant Rebels were produced, and while they never gained the cachet of the three-wheeled Reliant models, their influence would be felt again in the form of the Reliant Kitten, of which more later.

The later round pattern Smith's instruments were customised at manufacture to show the Reliant badge of the time.

The roomy engine bay allowed the Ford Escort engine to fit easily within as it did in a factory prototype that never made production.

A strange one-off vehicle was produced by Reliant in 1969. No doubt inspired by the sales of the sporting Scimitar range and their links with Ford UK (the Scimitar was powered by the Ford Essex V6 engine), the Rebel 1600 GT was fitted with a Ford 1600 crossflow engine as fitted to the Cortina 1600E, producing no less than 80 horsepower. It was a road legal vehicle but no records remain of how fast this prototype performed but figures of 204 horsepower per ton made it into print, which must have created a very fast Rebel indeed. People who were there considered it faster than the Scimitar and that it would have made an excellent addition to the Reliant sporting range. There was even talk of a fibreglass sports car body in the same vein as the MG Midget and Triumph Spitfire, but nothing got further than rough sketches. A shame, and an idea that would resurface again many years later.

5

Anadol

In 1965 the Otosan company of Turkey set in motion a plan to produce the first successful indigenous Turkish motorcar. An earlier attempt in the shape of the Devrim (meaning 'Revolution' in Turkish) only made it as far as the prototype stage, despite government backing and funding. Famously, one of the prototypes only made it 100 yards with the Turkish president inside at the Republic Day celebration parade in 1961 before breaking down.

The Otosan factory in Istanbul (established in a joint venture with Ford for this specific purpose) had produced the Ford Consul saloon since 1959, soon followed by the light commercial Ford Thames van. Spurred on by the Turkish government, Otosan found themselves speaking to Reliant to design a vehicle they could initially assemble from CKD (complete knocked down) kits with a view to taking more of the assembly and parts supply in-house as time passed. Reliant would christen this method of helping other countries start their own car production as offering them a 'Package motor industry'.

This official publicity photo of the Anadol (FW5 internally) clearly states UK production was planned, but never occurred.

Christened in advance the Anadol A1 (it was known as FW5 at Reliant, standing for four-wheeled model number five), Reliant commissioned their favourite designer Tom Karen of Ogle to design a handsome two-door saloon bodyshell for production in the Reliant trademark fibreglass. This was mounted on a separate chassis and was powered by the well-proven Ford Kent engine, initially in 1200 cc form, from the then current Ford Cortina, later updated to the stronger and more powerful 1300 cc version. This was mated to the well-proven Ford four-speed gearbox that offered a smooth and refined gear change. Unusually for the time, the clutch was hydraulically activated rather than the more conventional cable-operated design. This gave a smooth action to the clutch and was effectively self-adjusting as long as the fluid reservoir was kept topped up. The engine drove to the rear wheels through a Ford-sourced rear axle, all mounted on a sturdy 'H' shaped chassis frame.

Rear suspension was courtesy of leaf springs from the Ford Cortina. Like so many other limited productions cars, the front suspension was developed from the Triumph Herald/Spitfire system. Reliant were familiar with this system from their small Rebel saloon.

Specific thought had been given to a higher ride height than usual to allow for better ground clearance on the rough Turkish roads, and for tax reasons the weight of the final vehicle had to remain below 18 cwt.

The dashboard was simply appointed with two Smith's instrument clusters, one a speedometer and the other a large compound dial with small gauges for fuel level and water

This official photo of the specially built Otosan factory shows the scale of the enterprise. (Image courtesy of Jim Pace)

temperature. To keep the basic retail price low, the heater and radio were both optional extras. Unusually the handbrake only worked on one of the rear wheels, not both as is usual practice.

The Turkish government requested to see the prototype before they gave their approval for production and a roughly finished prototype was driven from Reliant in England to Turkey overland in December 1965. Reports claimed that the trip was completed in sixty-three hours by two drivers through adverse weather conditions, which proved the strength and integrity of the design.

The prototype was duly tested and approved by the Turkish government and production approved with the condition that it was in manufacture by the end of 1966. The prototypes were finished on 1 December 1966, and production began on 19 December following a swift but extensive testing programme.

The 1200 cc engine would give the Anadol A1 a claimed top speed of 79 miles per hour. The 0–60 miles per hour sprint was listed by the factory as 27 seconds. The later 1300 cc crossflow engine would increase the top speed to 84 miles per hour and remarkably reduce the 0–60 time to 16.7 seconds.

Reliant were contracted to supply all the drawings, moulds and training required to get the Anadol into production. They also acquired all the necessary parts from Ford UK and other suppliers and arranged for their shipping to the factory in Istanbul to allow

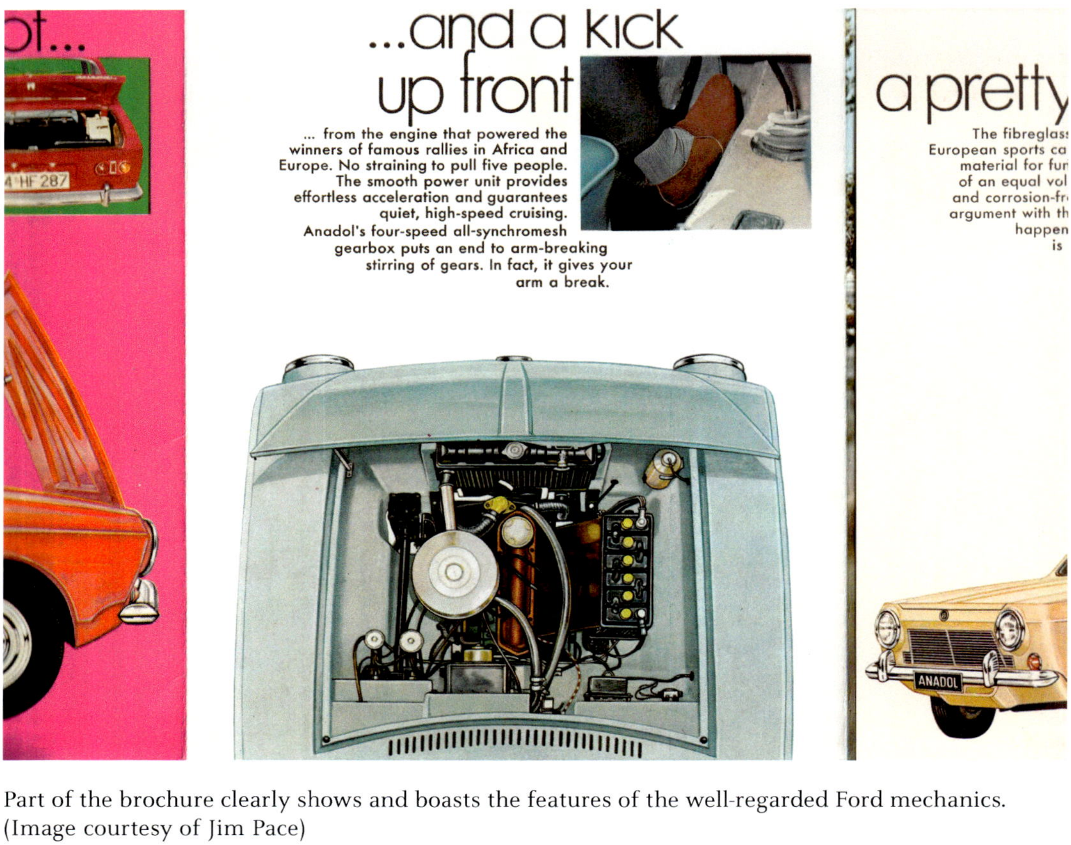

Part of the brochure clearly shows and boasts the features of the well-regarded Ford mechanics. (Image courtesy of Jim Pace)

the assembly of the vehicles. For this Reliant received a royalty of £200 for every Anadol produced.

In time Ford would supply their parts directly and buy out Reliant's royalty contract for a large but undisclosed sum. As production had risen to an unexpected level this was far cheaper for Otosan than continuing the royalty scheme that had previously been in place.

The sturdy basic design led to the Anadol A1 to be turned into Turkey's first rally car in 1968 as part of the newly established Anadol Ralli Takımı (Anadol Rally Team), winning the Thrace Rally, the first to be run in Turkey, in 1968, driven by Renc Kocibey and Demir Bukey. The long international history of tuning Ford engines gave the Anadol a head start over many other cars in the competition stakes. A copy of the historic 1968 car would come second in class in the 2010 Parking–Paris Rally, beaten only by an Aston Martin DB5.

The Anadol A1 had entered production in 1966, and when a new four-door body was introduced in 1973 it was the world's first production four-door fibreglass saloon.

Retail cost at launch was just over £1,000, which undercut many of the more mainstream products on the Turkish market. By 1967 the factory had to be extended to keep up with production demand and according to press material by 1968 'over 4000' vehicles were being produced per year.

Production of the Anadol A1 would continue until 1975, by which time nearly 20,000 had been produced. The four-door A2 would be produced until 1981 with many updates and would eventually have a production run of over 36,000 vehicles.

Reliant retained a tiny number of pick-up trucks in the UK (most sources say four examples) as service vehicles and a few have found their way back to the UK as personal

The brochure clearly shows the bold simplicity of the dashboard. (Image courtesy of Jim Pace)

imports converted to right-hand drive. At the time of writing two are believed to still exist in the UK, both in the process of being rebuilt.

A handful of press photos escaped the factory stating 'Later production is planned in Britain' in their captions, and a 1966 leaflet stated the FW5 design would be 'offered to other countries and later produced in the United Kingdom'. This never came to pass but must have been seriously considered.

The Turkish Anadol project came close to having another branch in New Zealand as the Anziel Nova, a prototype based on an imported Anadol kit that came via Reliant (the badges were changed to Reliant to facilitate this, even though there was never a Reliant version of the Anadol) to reduce import duties and was displayed in 1967.

The Anadol production line at Istanbul.

With a simple platform chassis beneath the fibreglass body the pick-up variant was easily developed. (Image courtesy of Jim Pace)

New Zealand entrepreneur Alan Gibbs announced his desire to produce the Anadol in New Zealand largely based on CKD kits from the UK with a target of producing around 3,000 per year. The government of the time, concerned with the balance of trade figures at the time (imports versus exports of a country), was actively seeking to reduce the number of vehicles being imported into New Zealand. Other importers were already having their quotas reduced, and eventually Gibbs was only allowed a permit to import the single example that would go on to become the prototype Anziel Nova.

Like the Turkish Anadol, the Anziel Nova was a two-door saloon, this time powered by a 1500 cc version of the Ford Kent engine. Plans to use the GT version in a later performance model were mentioned in press releases.

Gibbs fought back against proposed government restrictions with a claim that once production was underway he could raise the locally sourced content to 90 per cent, as Ford mechanics were already being produced in New Zealand, rather than continuing to import them from the UK.

The New Zealand government eventually relented and offered a licence to import 600 kits per year, but this was deemed insufficient to be a viable product and the plan was abandoned in 1970. Remarkably the sole prototype still exists.

The front of the parts manual shows the most common colour and the car's insignia top right. (Image courtesy of Jim Pace)

6

Scimitar

If there is one four-wheeled Reliant that most people have heard of it is the Scimitar. It was certainly their most famous four-wheeled vehicle, produced in larger numbers and for longer than any of their others.

Looking to update their earlier Sabra/Sabre model Reliant bought in the styling of the Ogle SX250 special. Ogle design had been commissioned by Boris Forter of Helena Rubenstein cosmetics to build a vehicle to his specific requirements and the Ogle SX250 was the result.

The styling was based on his own sketch, and he had chosen to use the smooth and torquey Edward Turner-designed Daimler V8 engine as the powerplant and the advanced Daimler Dart SP250 sports car chassis (hence the title SX250). As the body was to be built of lightweight fibreglass, the 2.5-litre version of the V8 engine was retained (a larger 4.5-litre version was available).

The Ogle SX250 made its debut at the 1962 Earls Court Motor Show and two examples were produced (there had been plans for six) before Ogle moved on to other projects.

A small Ogle-designed vehicle based on the Mini called the SX1000 was already in low-volume production at Ogle (sixty-six examples would be produced). This mounted Mini front and rear subframes on a streamlined fibreglass coupé bodyshell, the improved aerodynamics and lighter weight creating a small sporting car very different from the Mini that supplied the mechanical parts. Ogle had already approached Reliant with their extensive experience in producing fibreglass cars with a view to them producing it in greater numbers than their own facilities could manage. Reliant turned down this contract and instead bought the rights to the streamlined Ogle SX250 body style.

The body had to be extensively modified to fit on the Reliant Sabre chassis. The existing 2.5-litre Ford straight six-cylinder engine and matching Ford gearbox were retained for the new model.

Launched in 1964, the new coupé followed the sword-themed name of the Sabre and was named Scimitar GT, internally known as the SE4 (the SE code prefix came from using the first and last letters of the 'Sabre' model name). It proudly wore a chrome nose badge of the curved, heavy-bladed sword of the same name. The very first example would be registered as an Ogle and made the rounds of motoring magazines before production proper commenced.

The Ogle SX1000 Mini Coupé, the car that brought Ogle designs to Reliant.

Now tuned with triple SU carburettors and a custom-made Reliant gas-flowed exhaust manifold, the sturdy engine that had already found fame in the big Ford saloons produced 120 horsepower, which was sufficient to give a top speed of 117 miles per hour.

The rear suspension was revised after observations from experts in the motoring field considered the new, higher-output engine was 'too much' for the original system. The older Panhard rod system was replaced with an axle-mounted Watts linkage and twin trailing suspension arms.

The Watts linkage is a simple and compact way to locate the rear axle of a vehicle and its history goes back to the early days of vehicles (the patent was dated 1784), being named after the engineer James Watt, the same scientist after whom the unit of energy is christened. It allows a vehicle's rear axle to move easily up and down for comfort while preventing sideways motion that would adversely affect the handling.

Wire wheels were standard, as was a comfortable interior, a considerable step up from the more overtly sporting Sabre. In common with many other small-volume manufacturers of the time, the dashboard displayed a comprehensive set of instruments sat directly in front of the driver. Many mass-produced manufacturers still placed their instruments in the centre of the dashboard so the same dashboard could be used for both left- and right-hand-drive vehicles. Unusually for the time, an electric sunroof was available as an option.

Useful options available included the Laycock De Normanville overdrive. This was a form of electrically operated epicyclical gearing system that, once engaged, reduced the number of engine revolutions to allow more relaxed cruising and better fuel economy when used

Above: The Scimitar SE4 coupé was the model closest to the design of the original Ogle SX250. Wire wheels were standard.

Below: Plentiful proprietary rear lights and a Ford Consul bumper adorn the handsome lines of the rear of the coupé.

The SE4 followed the Reliant trend for well-equipped dashboards. Here the instruments were supplied by Smiths.

on the upper gears and better acceleration when used as a half-step between lower gears to create a simple and cheap close-ratio gearbox. On the Scimitar the overdrive worked on third and top gears. 296 straight six engine GT SE4 Scimitars would be produced before an update arrived for the 1966 season.

Ford Europe had for some time been laying plans for a family of mass-produced engines to power all their medium and large vehicles, along with commercial and marine applications. This would evolve into the 'Essex' family of V4 and V6 engines. A sturdy iron engine capable of withstanding hard use, the V6 version would claim to be the world's first mass-produced iron V6 engine. It would become available in both 2.5- and 3-litre capacities.

The passage of time would eventually reveal a weakness in the fibre teeth of the timing gear and in the slender oil pump drive shaft (known as the 'quill shaft') but otherwise a well-maintained example of the engine has been proven to last for many years. Fitted with the right exhaust system, it could also be relied upon to provide a suitably sporting exhaust note.

A V4 2-litre version of the engine was far less well received in the UK and quietly vanished from production after it was found to offer no advantages over the more conventional straight four-cylinder engines in the Ford range. A German version would gain a very different reputation for rugged longevity and would find its way under the bonnet of sporting SAABs as well as the now largely forgotten Ford Corsair saloon. In the UK it would be replaced by the long-lived Ford Pinto family of straight four-cylinder engines.

The sporting seats are comfortable and in keeping with the performance of the vehicle.

Always keen on the scale of manufacturing where greater figures led to a lower unit cost for an engine, Ford UK were actively seeking fresh customers for their new engines and they offered Reliant early examples to trial with the opportunity to purchase further examples at a generous trade discount.

Reliant adopted the 3-litre V6 version (as did their competitors Gilbern in South Wales) to create the new Scimitar SE4A. Considerably shorter than the straight six engine, Reliant took the opportunity to move the engine rearwards in the engine bay to improve the vehicle's weight distribution and handling. An anti-roll bar was fitted to tame the extra power and torque of the V6 engine and general strengthening was carried out to the front chassis frame.

The higher torque generated by the V6 engine allowed for the fitting of a higher-ratio rear axle for more relaxed high-speed cruising, even more so if the optional overdrive unit was specified. Sadly the extra torque and horsepower meant that the classic-look wire wheels could no longer be offered as they lacked strength and had to be replaced by stronger, wider steel wheels.

Inside, the dashboard was updated with black-rimmed instruments and an 'anti-dazzle' finish for other parts. Extra padding was strategically fitted to offer protection to the occupants in the event of an accident. A hunt around the Ford parts bins also gave Reliant moveable dashboard air vents to direct hot and cold air around the passenger cabin, a first for the Reliant range.

Four instruments were placed directly in front of the driver: a large rev counter and a speedometer flanking smaller water temperature and oil pressure gauges. Three smaller gauges were placed in the centre of the dashboard (a fuel gauge, an ammeter and a clock).

Early coupés were powered by the 2.5-litre Ford straight six-cylinder engine.

The press said nice things of the new V6 Scimitar at launch in 1965, and to broaden the appeal of the Scimitar in 1967 the new cheaper GT SE4C would adopt the smaller 2.5-litre version of the Essex engine. Visually differing only in the badge on the rear, it was still capable of 110 miles per hour while offering marginally better fuel economy.

118 of these lower-powered Scimitars were produced before the whole coupé range was withdrawn in 1970, alongside around 600 of the 3-litre version.

For 1968 Reliant would introduce a groundbreaking new Scimitar that would introduce what was arguably a whole new concept: the sporting estate car.

Tom Karen was asked to produce an adaption of the Ogle design experimental GTS estate car that would be suitable to be fitted to the Scimitar chassis to create a full four-seat estate production version. The GTS was originally created as a showpiece for Triplex heated glass. It would spend two years as the personal car of the late Prince Phillip and then spend many years as a permanent exhibit at Beaulieu motor museum.

In later years on speaking tours Tom Karen would admit that the Scimitar was his favourite design. Specifically, he would point out the upswing in the swage line below the rear windows as his favourite design feature of all time. Now a common feature on many of the current ranges of SUVs and estate cars, Tom Karen used it first on the Scimitar.

Christened the SE5 GTE (grand touring estate), this new sporting estate design was launched at the 1968 Motor Show. Extensive work had been necessary to turn the design into a production reality. A new, longer chassis was designed to accommodate the hatch-accessed estate load area, the latter made larger by having the spare wheel moved

Left: The launch of the groundbreaking Scimitar GTE in 1968 as trumpeted by this contemporary 1969 poster for the Motor Show.

Below: The Scimitar SE5 GTE launched the basic shape for all the Scimitars that followed after.

under the bonnet. This move also allowed for the fitting of the larger than expected fuel tank under the flat load area of the estate bed.

The new chassis allowed a longer suspension travel which improved the ride, especially when heavy loads were being carried. The GTE had 8 inches of suspension travel where the more sporting coupé made do with 5.5 inches.

A sturdy steel roll-over hoop was moulded into the fibreglass bodyshell and then bolted directly onto the chassis behind the B pillars to provide protection to any occupants in the unlikely event of a complete inversion of the car.

Inside there were now two genuine rear seats rather than what had been effectively a padded shelf in the rear of the Scimitar coupé. The rear wheel arches did not intrude into the new rear load area, and both rear seats could be folded flat to create the ultimate amount of flat luggage space. The two seats could be folded separately to offer a choice of load-carrying capacities and shape. Many consider Reliant to be the inventers of the 'split fold' seat system now seen in almost every modern hatchback.

Thoughtfully, Reliant fitted a light that illuminated the rear load area for loading in the dark, a feature repeated under the bonnet.

Reinforcing the long-distance touring character of the car, the petrol tank had a capacity of 17 imperial gallons, slightly down on the Scimitar coupé but still offering a touring range of around 400 miles with the optional overdrive.

The 3-litre Ford Essex V6 was carried over from the coupé model offering a 120 miles per hour top speed with the 0–60 miles per hour sprint being covered in 10.2 seconds, a little up from the 9.9 seconds recorded for the coupé.

The live Salisbury rear axle continued to be located by the tried and tested system of pairs of trailing arms, coil springs and a Watts linkage. The new sturdy front suspension was created from Triumph TR6 uprights and wishbones, with a steering rack taken from an Austin 1800 and brakes from a Jaguar XJ6.

The Ford Zodiac four-speed gearbox was retained and the overdrive option remained popular. For 1970 a three-speed automatic option became available at no extra cost.

Designer Tom Karen would claim in later interviews that the rising waistline of the GTE rear window was his favourite design flourish. It is copied today by SUVs everywhere.

The Reliant Scimitar was the world's first production car to offer Wolfrace wheels as an option.

Like many other small manufacturers using this manual gearbox, the huge gap in ratios between first/second and third/forth attracted adverse comment, but with the abundant torque available from the 3-litre V6 engine in general use, it was far less of an issue than the contemporary road tests would have you believe. Without the optional Laycock De Normanville overdrive the top gear offered 20 miles per hour per thousand engine revolutions, and with overdrive this leapt to a much more relaxing 24.6 miles per thousand revolutions, with the attendant savings in fuel.

Motor magazine recorded a touring fuel consumption figure of 27.9 miles per gallon, which was considered not unreasonable for a sporting car of the era. A rather less impressive overall road test figure of just over 19 miles per gallon was recorded for their whole 1,200 miles test. *Motor* spoke highly of the comfort and refinement of the Scimitar GTE and considered it capable of easily cruising at 100 miles per hour using the overdrive top gear.

A true trendsetter, the estate would inspire fellow fibreglass manufacturer and direct competitors Gilbern in South Wales to add an estate to their Invader saloon range. A popular model from launch in 1971, it never achieved the national sales success of the Scimitar and never made it into their revised Invader series 3 in 1972.

For 1972 the already popular design was updated and christened the SE5B. Revisions to the Essex V6 engine gave a small 7 horsepower power increase and the earlier Ford Zodiac gearbox was replaced with one from a Ford Capri. Reliant fitted this with their own custom-made rear casting and output shaft unique to the Scimitar. The gear change linkage was sourced from the German version of the Ford Capri. Coupled with the standard overdrive, the new ratios allowed a very relaxed and economical cruising gait of only 2,700 rpm at 70 miles per hour. This gave a remarkable touring fuel consumption in overdriven top gear of no less than 28.2 miles per gallon, with a more expected 21.7 miles per gallon in general use. With the 17-gallon tank, it offered a range of around 480 miles.

Reliant claimed a top speed of 123 miles per hour for the SE5B, and *Motor* magazine managed a 0–60 sprint in 8.7 seconds. Their 0–100 miles per hour figure of 27.7 seconds was outstanding for a car of the Scimitar's size and style.

The Scimitar SE5 retained the four-headlight nose with less of a pointed section between them, and cut and shut Ford-sourced quarter bumpers replaced the earlier full-width versions.

Once again Reliant updated the interior to offer a new-look dashboard with repositioned air vents and heater controls. Electric windows became available and there was a change to the rear light units.

In total 9,416 SE5 series Scimitar GTEs were produced, outselling the coupé by a reported ratio of 4:1 at the time. Production was running at around seventy vehicles per week by this point.

Their most famous owner would be Princess Anne, who was given a Scimitar GTE by her parents, Queen Elizabeth II and Prince Philip, Duke of Edinburgh, for her twentieth birthday in 1970. Finished in RAF blue with a light blue interior, it would come with the personal registration of 1420H in recognition of her position as Colonel in Chief of the 14th/20th Hussars. She would go on to own several more, and purchase many smaller Reliants for use on her estates.

Reliant took the Scimitar range upmarket in 1975 when they launched the SE6 range. The new model was 2 inches wider and 4 inches longer than the SE5, which massively increased the interior space, particularly for passengers riding in the rear seats. The seats, often velour coated as was the fashion at the time, were considered comfortable by almost all road testers. Luggage space was also increased, more through width than depth of the load area. The fuel tank would grow to 20 gallons, further enhancing the already long range of the Scimitar by offering a theoretical range of over 500 miles. The estate load area offered no less than 595 litres of space, this being nearly doubled if the rear seats were folded.

Above: New rear lights from the Ford parts bin updated the rear of the GTE, and the opening hatch vastly increased the practicality of the design.

Below: A black dashboard replaced the wood look of the earlier version, the instruments remaining largely the same.

The dashboard continued to offer a full range of instruments in a black dashboard. The large engine rev counter and speedometer were placed in front of the driver with the traditional four small dials at the top of the centre console. Below these sat a smart analogue clock. All offered a clear display of easily read information about speed of progress and engine condition, but some road tests commented the design now looked dated.

An array of warning lights were replaced by a warning light cluster from the upmarket Triumph saloon range, which put all the warning lights a car would ever need in a single, clearly labelled circle directly in front of the driver.

The front suspension was by an independent wishbone and coil spring system. At the rear the live axle was located by the long-standing system of coil springs and radius arms on an axle located by the Watts linkage.

The front of the car was facelifted with a new bumper, and the outer pair of the four headlights were now of a larger diameter than the inner pair. Previously all four headlights had been of the same size, and the new setup was described in one road test as offering 'penetrating night-time illumination'.

The door handles were changed from the traditional 'press buton to open' Ford Cortina type to an award-winning flush fitting type from the Morris Marina (they would also be found in the Robin and Kitten). These classic handles would find their way onto the doors of an incredible range of exotic vehicles from the likes of Lotus and would remain current at Rover for many years, the last vehicle introduced using them being the first model Land Rover Discovery.

This Reliant press photograph highlights the high roofline and profile of their new GTE.

The SE6 was replaced by the updated SE6A in 1976 after 543 examples had been manufactured. The changes were many, small and frequently hard to see (the front grille and badging being the most visibly obvious) but included the adoption of superior Lockheed brakes and a general revision of the suspension for improved handling and comfort. The rear drum brakes were now larger than before, while the front discs were smaller but more efficient.

Road tests reported an excellent set of performance figures for an estate car. The top speed was recorded as 118 miles per hour and the 0–60 time as 9.6 seconds.

No fewer than 3,877 Scimitar SE6As were produced before circumstances forced a major overhaul for the 1980 season and the announcement of the Scimitar SE6B.

Having been in full production in a range of forms since the late 1960s, Ford ceased production of the Essex V6 engine in the early 1980s in favour of the German-developed Cologne V6 as their family V6 engine.

With a capacity of 2.8 litres, it had similar displacement but a slightly lower power output than the older Essex V6 engine, albeit delivered in a more refined way. On the credit side, the new Cologne V6 was no less than 40 pounds lighter than the outgoing Iron Essex V6, which helped to offset the power deficit.

The last generation Essex V6 engines delivered 144 horsepower where the new Cologne V6 produced 135. It also produced less torque but was a far freer revving engine. This

Scimitar GTE: Reliant grand tourer/estate. Four seats; 120 mph; automatic option for 1970.

This 1970 press photograph highlights the GTE's performance and the new automatic option for 1970. Note Reliant's own pattern wheels.

forced Reliant to fit the new generation Scimitar SE6B with a lower ratio rear axle to maintain the acceleration and sporty feel of their product. This reduced the refinement at speed (something for which it was famed) and increased fuel consumption. In fairness to this fact that is often quoted in modern reviews of the Scimitar range, both *Autocar* and *Motor* reviews in 1980 considered the refinement of the Scimitar family to be excellent, with conversations possible with raised voices not being needed up to a cruising speed of 70 miles per hour.

Usually supplied fitted with fuel injection on Ford models, Reliant decided to avoid the expense and effort associated with updating what was by now an ageing design. There was space aplenty under the bonnet (despite the continuing presence of the spare wheel) for an injection system, but Reliant retained a carburettor fuel system.

Transmission remained the faithful Ford four-speed gearbox with a standard Laycock De Normanville overdrive or a three-speed Ford automatic gearbox. On the luxury front electric door mirrors would come as standard, as would halogen headlights, an updated front spoiler and side rubbing strips.

Production of the SE6B would end in 1980 after 407 examples had been manufactured.

Running alongside the famous GTE range from 1980 Reliant also produced the rather lesser-remembered GTC (Grand Touring Convertible).

Scimitar GTE: A view of the 1970 model showing the rear wiper and washer.

Also new for 1970, Reliant made much of the new rear wiper.

Down in South Wales Gilbern were inspired by the success of their competitors at Reliant to design their own sporting estate. Barely 200 were sold.

Aimed at what the media described as the Triumph Stag market (the Triumph Stag had ceased production in 1977), Reliant had once again commissioned Tom Karen to create a design study for a large convertible using existing Scimitar running gear.

Early prototypes featured the then current Ford Essex engine, but by the time the GTC entered production the Cologne V6 had been adopted and the new GTC bodyshell sat on a chassis borrowed from the newly launched SE6B Scimitar range.

The Triumph Stag parts bin fittingly donated its hood frame and roll-over bar, and the sturdy separate chassis made the car more refined and far less prone to flexing than many of its convertible contemporaries.

Now the strength of the roof had been removed torsional rigidity was enhanced by strengthening tubes running off the roll cage. There was also a strengthening tube that braced the front bulkhead/facia mounting to the transmission tunnel frame and new, sturdier mounting bars for the door hinges. Previous experience had taught Reliant that after a period of the time the large doors, even though made of lighter fibreglass, had a tendency to 'droop' on their hinges.

Under the skin there were many detail changes largely common to the SE6B. A revised propeller shaft with a centre bearing took the power from the new Cologne V6 to the new, lower-ratio rear axle. This took advantage of the newer, higher-revving character of the new Cologne engine but still offered a reasonably high-cruising gear ratio of 26.5 miles per hours for every thousand engine revolutions.

Suspension settings were all updated to offer a more sporting ride and handling, and the rear suspension mounting points were moved to enhance the handling and to give more room in the boot. Some road tests appreciated the sporting ride and handling, while others

The facelifted SE6 introduced larger outer headlights to the established GTE front end.

felt the stiff ride that offered the sports car handling detracted from the large convertible refinement they expected.

The standard power steering system was updated to offer more feel through the steering wheel for enthusiastic drivers, while a lower-geared manual, unassisted steering system was an option.

Outside the unchanged Scimitar GTE nose gained a new spoiler to improve aerodynamics and stability at speed. The hood was considered a good fit by road testers of the time and did little to detract from the refinement of the hard-roofed GTE. A hardtop would soon join the options list.

Motor magazine tested the Scimitar GTC in 1980 and recorded a top speed of 114 miles per hour and a 0–60 time of 9.7 seconds. They found 117 miles per hour were possible in what they described as 'favourable conditions'. They recorded a combined fuel consumption figure of 23.7 miles per gallon and a touring fuel consumption of 27.4 miles per gallon. These were considered excellent for what they described as a 'heavy 2.8 litre sports car'.

Without the rear estate body the GTC weighed considerably less than the GTE (some sources say by as much as 10 per cent), so both performance and economy were considered good for its class. Those still wanting extra luggage space could still fold down the rear seats in an option carried over from the GTE and extend the luggage area over the space usually occupied by the rear seats.

Many road tests of the time spoke favourably of both the refinement and handling of the GTC and no fewer than 340 were sold in 1980. At launch the price was already high at £1,1360, and inflation would press the price higher over the next few years.

Sadly both fashion and a recession made such large touring cars less popular, and Reliant did not have a name and reputation of the likes of Mercedes to support their expensive cars through the recession.

Scimitar GTE: The Borg Warner 35 automatic gearbox, offered as an optional extra for 1970.

1970 brought the option of automatic transmission to the GTE range.

Only three examples found homes in 1981, twenty in 1982, twenty-four in 1983, twenty-nine in 1984 and thirteen per year in 1985 and 1986.

Reliant ceased production of the now ageing Scimitar range in 1986, but the Scimitar would rise again.

Two Lucas employees, Peter Boam and John McCauley, with close links to Reliant were aware that production was soon going to end and that there were still unfulfilled orders on the books. They approached racing car company Middlebridge with an offer.

Middlebridge had been set up by wealthy Japanese publisher and Anglophile Kohji Nakauchi and ex-Aston Martin manager Dennis Nursey in 1986 to run a racing team in the UK. Successful in both the Formula 2000 and Formula 3000 classes, they purchased Brabham in 1990 with the aim of taking on the Formula One world.

Alongside their racing teams both men had been watching the steady flow of traditional British cars being exported to Japan and were looking to build something similar themselves for the export market. When Boam and McCauley approached them with an already sealed deal to buy the Scimitar production rights (they had planned to build a whole new factory in Northampton) it looked like an excellent shortcut to their goal of building a unique British motorcar. Middlebridge took control of the production tools in 1987.

They updated the Scimitar to use the latest 2.9-litre fuel-injected version of the Ford Cologne V6 engine producing 150 horsepower and marketed the car as a hand-built, luxury model. Middlebridge would claim at the time that the Scimitar was the world's fastest production estate car with a top speed of 120 miles per hour and a 0–60 time of 7.5 seconds.

No fewer than ten layers of paint were claimed to be applied to every example, and a huge range of new and adventurous colours were announced including pearlescent finishes. Sound-proofing was improved and luxurious leather featured strongly in the interior. The press release at the time reported no fewer than 450 changes and improvements had been

Above: This 1972 press photo shows the new taillights for that model year.

Below: The light weight of the GTE and the tuning potential of the Ford Essex engine soon saw them in use as competition cars.

The warning light cluster that was a feature of later Scimitar dashboards in its original location, the dashboard of the Triumph 1300.

made to the original design before the new Scimitar was eventually launched at the 1989 Motor Show.

The suspension was revised to enhance handling and comfort, and for longevity a galvanised chassis frame was introduced. Much was made in the press of a planned production capacity of 300 cars per year, but such figures were never achieved.

As their best-known owner, Princess Anne opened the factory at Lilac Grove in Beeston, Nottingham, in October 1988 and would purchase the fifth example produced for her own use. It was in this car that she would receive speeding tickets so widely reported in the UK press. She received two, on the same day, from the same constable. She would retain her beloved Middlebridge Scimitar until 2023 in the absence of finding a suitable replacement.

Under a strange system, despite having sold the production rights and moulds of the Scimitar to Middlebridge, Reliant were still producing the bodies under contract for the Middlebridge Scimitars. These were shipped still awaiting curing to the Beeston factory, where they would receive what was claimed to be 200 hours of work for finishing, assembly and painting to produce the 'hand-made luxury' they claimed.

Production of the Middlebridge Scimitar would run for seventy-seven cars (one would be a prototype GTC) before production ceased again in 1990. The rights changed hands yet again and a few more examples were produced by a smaller company owned by Graham Walker, a confessed Scimitar enthusiast and now owner of arguably the UK's largest

Above: The Scimitar GTC. The last of the Scimitars introduced, it deserved more success than it achieved.

Right: Boot space was liberated in all Scimitars by storing the spare wheel under the bonnet where it also provided some measure of extra protection in the event of an accident.

Scimitar specialist. At the time of writing the production rights, along with the moulds and jigs required for production, remain in his possession.

Despite many optimistic reports in the media, the Scimitar would not rise again.

Over the long career in production, the Scimitar family of cars sold no fewer than 14,273 examples of all models and they remain a common and popular sight at classic car shows.

Above: The dashboard of the Scimitar SE6B (seen here on a GTC) was considered dated by some reviewers but many considered it a classic of clear design.

Left: The rear seats of the GTC (see her in optional leather) were surprisingly roomy.

7

Kitten and Fox

The launch of the Reliant Robin three-wheeler led to a huge leap in production numbers for the Reliant company. It was the model which made them famous all over the world and the model everyone thought of when the name Reliant was mentioned. From the launch in 1973, every three-wheeled Reliant would come to be called Robin by onlookers, helped by Birmingham-born comedian Jasper Carrott, who made the three-wheeler the butt of many jokes over the years, even if he would insist on referring to the vehicle as the 'Robin Reliant'.

When production of the new Robin took off so unexpectedly production of the older Reliant Rebel was halted to allow them to concentrate all their resources on their new product.

Production of the Rebel ended in 1974, by which time it was a dated-looking design, but not before it had been used as a production test bed for the new 850 cc version of the Reliant engine. Never a huge seller, it did attract a new clientele to Reliant, and company

The cover of the Reliant Kitten brochure at launch.

owner Ray Wiggin was keen to have a small four-wheeled Reliant in the range that might attract people moving up from the three-wheeled range. It might also attract people who liked but could not afford the large Scimitar, or maybe even as a second car to a Scimitar owner. The result was the Reliant Kitten.

Again styled by Ogle design, the new Kitten was launched in 1975. As with the Rebel, one of the requirements of the design was that it should keep as many parts common to the Reliant Robin as possible – body and mechanical.

Early prototypes were considered visually too similar to the Robin, so changes were made to the front. A new full-width black grille, square headlights from the Hillman Avenger and black bumper covers were all added. The rear was identical to the Robin with the exception of black bumper covers. There was a full-length black coach line along the waistline of the vehicle and both publicity pictures and sales brochures at launch would show optional alloy wheels on the saloon version.

Unlike most cars of the era the small bonnet was hinged forwards towards the front bumper rather than back towards the passenger compartment.

Reliant Kitten 850cc Estate: 40 cubic feet capacity (with seats down) and up to 60mpg.

This launch publicity photo placed the new Kitten estate by the Landseer lion sculptures (named after their sculptor) in Trafalgar Square.

Reliant Kitten: a hand-built 850cc saloon capable of up to 60mpg and 80mph.

This launch publicity photo of the Reliant Kitten saloon features the seldom seen optional alloy wheels and clearly shows the rear common to the Robin three-wheeler.

In common with the Robin and Rebel, the Kitten was available as both a saloon and an estate car. The saloon shared the rounded rear styling of the Robin saloon with a self-latching vertically opening rear window. The estate had a taller, squarer profile and a side-opening rear door as pioneered by the Reliant Rebel. The publicity material for the estate at launch boasted of 40 cubic feet of carrying capacity with the seats folded.

Power came from the latest version of the 850 cc Reliant engine as used in the Robin but helpfully mounted further which made maintenance far easier It was tuned to give 40 horsepower and breathed through an efficient SU carburettor. This power output was sufficient to give the Kitten a top speed of 'nearly eighty miles per hour' according to the press release while still retaining a claimed 60 plus miles per gallon, no doubt helped by the light weight of the vehicle.

The captions of publicity photographs for the time would claim a full 80 miles per hour. Sadly road testers would find the claimed 60 miles per gallon economy hard to replicate, most finding figures between 43 and 46 miles per gallon in general use.

The top speed given in the press handout at the launch of the Reliant Kitten was 77 miles per hour, with a top gear ratio of a decently refined 17 miles per hour for every 1,000 engine revolutions.

The benchmark 0–60 miles per hour sprint was given as being covered in a reasonable 15.4 seconds. Contemporary road tests would find a slightly higher figure of just over 16 seconds. Unlike the Rebel, there was no compromise in performance or mechanical refinement with the Kitten; it could hold its head up alongside most of the competition.

A black grille and bumper covers were applied late in the design stage to make the Kitten look more different than the Robin.

The interior was common with the Robin except for the centre of the car where a new trim section was required to accommodate the different position of the gear lever. The upholstery could be had in black or brown and reclining seats were a standard fitment.

The front suspension of the Rebel had been derived from that of the Triumph Herald, and was retained, updated and brought completely in-house by Reliant for the Kitten, now using their own double wishbone system and in view of the extra performance available from the new engine, an anti-roll bar. The rear suspension remained as it was on the Robin, with a live axle and suspension by leaf springs.

Inspired by what had come before and the excellent handling it offered, the new system endowed the car with a tiny turning circle of 23 feet, less even than the fabled London black cab taxi.

A luxury version arrived in 1976 labelled the Kitten DL with an interior inspired by the successful Scimitar sporting range that included velour seats in black or brown. There were also amendments to the front suspension and a larger anti-roll bar to improve the handling of what was a surprisingly sprightly vehicle.

With the production capacity issues caused by the huge success of the Reliant Robin addressed, for 1977 Reliant could manage to launch the 6 cwt Kitten van – effectively a Kitten estate car without the side window apertures cut out and with more hard-wearing plastic upholstery (the passenger seat was optional). As with the Rebel, a side window kit

Above: The Kitten estate was designed with high, square roofline to make the best of the stowage space available given the size of the vehicle.

Below: The Kitten DL featured luxurious velour seats facing a clear dashboard. Much was in common with the three-wheeled Robin – only the position of the gear lever clearly gives away that this is a Kitten.

was available from Reliant dealers for owners to fit themselves, or at least have fitted after the vehicle had been registered as a van with the attendant saving in tax.

The van came fitted with round headlights common to the Robin as they were cheaper than the square versions fitted to the Kitten. Around 400 were produced.

Production of the Reliant Kitten ended in 1982 and had been a more successful product than the earlier Rebel, with production totalling over 4,500 vehicles.

Well after production had officially ended Reliant found themselves with a stock of surplus chassis and bodyshells which dealers could purchase as a kit of parts to assemble as new vehicles. Some private owners also took this route into new Kitten ownership, with the practice carrying on as late as 1985/86. Mix and match parts were a feature of these 'kits', and they can be recognised today by their 'Q' prefix number plates.

But like so many Reliant vehicles produced in the UK, the story did not end when production ceased at Bradford in 1982. A deal was struck with Sipani Autos of Bangalore in India to assemble the Reliant Kitten under the name of the Dolphin from Reliant-manufactured CKD kits. Sales were limited as two-door cars had never been popular in India and some Indian states actually required that all cars that carry four people must have separate doors for the rear passengers.

Later a four-door version was developed, known as the Montana, production of which would run until 1990. Curiously the mechanical parts and chassis would live on after 1990 when Sipani updated the bodyshell by effectively making a fibreglass copy of the Daihatsu Charade bodyshell and fitting it to the Kitten chassis and marketing it as the D-1.

In common with the Rebel predecessor, the rear door of the Kitten estate was side hinged, took up the whole rear of the vehicle and opened onto huge luggage space, increased further by fold-down rear seats.

Above: The four-wheel configuration allowed the engine to be moved forward making servicing tasks far easier.

Below: Reliant sales and marketing director Roger Musgrave (fourth from left) shows off the new Reliant Kitten at the Motor Show.

Greek company MEBEA had assembled three-wheeled Reliants for many years for their native Greek market, and they marketed a small utility vehicle using the Reliant Kitten chassis and running gear under a new fibreglass body developed for them by Reliant. It had removable rear seats, an optional hard top for the loading bed and a basic interior.

Reliant showed the vehicle alongside their own products at the 1980 British Motor show and were sufficiently inspired by the feedback they received to consider the product for the UK market. It was launched at the 1982 British Motor Show as the Reliant Fox and reached the dealers in 1983. A press release optimistically described the sturdy utilitarian styling as 'cheerfully impertinent'.

Under the new pick-up fibreglass body the chassis and 850 cc 40 horsepower engine remained unchanged. Unlike the Reliant Kitten, the chassis was advertised as being galvanised for rust resistance.

Officially the Reliant Fox could reach 74 miles per hour and cover the 0–60 benchmark in 22 seconds unladen.

The Fox was supplied as standard with a folding tilt cover for the load bed with a fold-up rear window. The tailgate was removable and the carrying capacity was advertised as 7 cwt. Advertised options included a removable rear seat, a fibreglass hardtop and an infill panel behind the front seats to create a full pick-up truck.

The Kitten-based Reliant Fox pick-up started life as a design for MEBEA in Greece introduced to the UK market after interest shown at the UK Motor Show.

The Greek MAEBA factory showing their three-wheeled Reliant-based utility vehicle output. As the sign clearly shows, they also assembled vehicles for German Zundap.

Around 600 would find homes before production ceased in 1990. Rumours at the time said that production had actually ceased in 1987 (Lucas parts manuals and the Parkers car guide support this rumour) when emissions from the engine became an issue. Emissions were not tested or fuel economy figures officially collated for three-wheeled vehicles, so production of the engine would continue for their use exclusively.

8

Metrocab

The iconic FX4 London black cab is known all over the world and is an integral part of the London scenery. Enjoying a near monopoly on the Taxi (more correctly the Hackney carriage) trade, by the time production ceased in 1997 it was a dated and archaic design with a reputation for going rusty and with poor quality control.

The rules governing the Hackney carriage trade (specifically, the Metropolitan Police Conditions of Fitness for London taxicabs) are old-fashioned in the extreme, with regulations in place about gentlemen being able to board and alight while wearing a top hat. Any vehicle hoping to be accepted by the regulatory body would have to be designed with their co-operation (if not actual assistance) to have a chance of being accepted for use in London.

Metrocab started life as a purpose-built design to take on the famous Austin FX4 London black cab. (Photo courtesy of D & B auto spares, Chard)

When the Austin FX3 taxi was available (1948–58) it faced competition from the Beardmore cab, which was a similar design, at one stage accounting for nearly half of London taxi sales. Austin worked hard to make their product better and to offer superior support for their FX3. When Beardmore production ended in 1966 the Austin products (now the iconic FX4) ruled unchallenged for many years.

Metro-Cammel-Weymann coachbuilders of Birmingham, more famous for their range of bus bodies, had constructed the last of the Beardmore range and sought to produce a replacement to keep their production lines running. Their initial design ideas were first seen in 1970 but the final product did not reach production until 1987.

The tall fibreglass bodyshell was designed with a very low floor to allow easy access for seven passengers, both fully mobile and in wheelchairs, the latter in anticipation of proposed new rules that would make wheelchair access a requirement of all new London taxis. The Metrocab would be the first dedicated taxi design to offer this feature.

Like many limited production vehicles, the parts bins of larger manufacturers were the source of many of the parts used.

The grille, headlights and indicators were sourced from the Ford Granada and the rear lights from the then current Ford Escort Cabriolet (Ford always being happy to sell parts to outside manufacturers). The dashboard and interior switchgear was bought in from Austin Rover family of cars, much like on the small Reliant sports car the SS1. Wing mirrors were sourced from the Ford Granada.

The dashboard was sourced from the Rover group parts bins in common with the SS1 sports car. (Photo courtesy of D & B auto spares, Chard)

The high, square profile made access easy for passengers. (Photo courtesy of D & B auto spares, Chard)

Under the bonnet lay the indestructible Ford Transit 2.5-litre diesel direct injection engine mated to a Ford automatic gearbox. The latter would lead to Metrocab being far cheaper to service than the Austin FX4.

To ensure the bodywork matched the longevity of the mechanics (a huge sore point with London taxi drivers, the FX4 being rust prone) the chassis was galvanised and the bodyshell was to be made from fibreglass. This lighter bodyshell also made the Metrocab more economical to run. Which is where Reliant initially came in. As the world's foremost and largest users of fibreglass for vehicle applications, they were involved in the production of the bodies from the start.

The Reliant-designed bodyshell offered such a low-level floor that wheelchair users could often enter the vehicle without assistance from a moderate kerb height while lightweight ramps were stowed away in a dedicated holder in the boot for when no kerb was available. Remote locking to position the wheelchair was operated by the driver to ensure a wheelchair would not move about during the journey, even during unexpected abrupt movements. To further aid access the side doors of Metrocab opened to a full 90 degrees from the body.

Mindful of the likelihood of body damage during use the Reliant-designed body used bolt-on panels for the most vulnerable panels such as the doors, bumpers and wings.

When Metro-Cammell-Weymann (part of the lager Laird group) had to sell the taxi manufacturing part of their business empire in 1989 due to debts run up during their

The passenger access doors of Metrocab were designed to open to a full 90 degrees from the body for easy access for both mobile and disabled passengers. (Photo courtesy of D & B auto spares, Chard)

involvement in the Channel Tunnel project the production rights were purchased by Reliant and the production line move to their factory in Tamworth. They adopted an updated version of the Ford diesel engine and added a manual gearbox to the options list, but the product remained otherwise largely unchanged.

Production was slow to get underway at the Tamworth site and at one stage there were newspaper reports of frustrated Taxi drivers storming into the Reliant works demanding to know why vehicle and parts orders were taking so long to be supplied. Reliant blamed a shortage of manpower and problems with parts supplies but assured them that full production of all things would soon be underway.

Like most of their cars, as an essentially handmade product it was not cheap (around £17,000 on introduction) but so good was their work and the product that many remained in active taxi service for over twenty years. At one point between 25 and 30 per cent of taxi sales in London would be the Metrocab.

One of Reliant's most unusual customers for Metrocab was an Australian taxi company in Sydney. They ordered 200 Metrocabs less their drivetrains. Once delivered they were fitted with locally produced LPG-fuelled Holden engines with matching gearboxes and rear axles.

A new version named the Metrocab TTT was launched in 2000 with a claimed 700 improvements. With financial troubles of their own, Reliant had sold the rights to Hooper's coachbuilders in 1991, although they continued to produce the bodyshells at Tamworth.

Above left: Metrocab was the first taxi to offer wide door openings, a flat floor and a securing system for wheelchair passengers. (Photo courtesy of D & B auto spares, Chard)

Above right: A first among taxis, all Metrocabs came with ramps for wheelchair access, and the flat floor allowed direct access from many high kerbs. (Photo courtesy of D & B auto spares, Chard)

Hooper's continued production of the Metrocab for nine years before finally selling the rights to a Singapore-based company called Kamkorp in 2000 and production would run until 2004. When the Metrocab production finally ended in 2004 it would cost Reliant one hundred jobs at their already struggling Tamworth factory where they were still producing the bodies.

The Metrocab name would rise again with British company Frazer-Nash as a zero-emissions taxi that attracted attention all around the world (it even merited an entry in the Australian daily newspaper *The Australian* in 2014), but despite the backing of then London Mayor Boris Johnson and plans for production to begin in 2016, the project foundered in 2018 when Frazer-Nash were 'wound up' by court order due to their debts.

9

The Bond Connection

Always a deadly rival in the three-wheeled market, Bond had been producing arguably more advanced three-wheeled cars than Reliant since 1949, at Preston in Lancashire, based on a design by Laurie Bond. Later owned by Sharps commercials, during the 1960s they would produce the four-wheeled Equipe range. This was effectively created by fitting a largely fibreglass body (the original steel doors and bulkhead were retained) on Triumph Herald and Vitesse chassis frames to create a handsome range of small coupés and convertibles. These were viewed sufficiently favourably by Triumph that they were made available through their dealership chain.

When the Hillman Imp-powered Bond 875 three-wheeler raised the spectre of eating into the sales of Reliant's three-wheeled range they bought Bond in 1969.

Bizarrely the Bond 875 would be used as the basis for the Jon Pertwee *Doctor Who* 'Whomobile', a streamlined vehicle first seen in the 1974 story 'Invasion of the Dinosaurs'. It would later be shown in Jon Pertwee's last *Doctor Who* story 'Plant of the Spiders' in flight through the use of special effects. It still exists today and regularly tours the UK fan conventions.

Among other benefits, the management at Reliant were eyeing the prospect of selling updated versions of their own four-wheeled vehicles through the Triumph dealership chain badged as Bonds.

Their planned product got as far as the prototype body stage when disaster struck. Just as the purchase of Bond was finalised Standard-Triumph became part of the motoring behemoth that was British Leyland, who had no interest in continuing the previous arrangement Standard-Triumph had with Bond.

So the Bond name did not die and hoping to retain their sporting reputation Reliant created the Bond Bug with an eye towards the youth market.

Officially only available only in bright orange (a colour chosen as it was the cheapest paint available), a handful of green and six white examples were produced, the former as part of a Robinson's jam promotion, the latter promoting Rothmans cigarettes. The Bug was at least spiritually a descendant of the Bond 875.

It was usually powered by the then new 750 cc version of the Reliant engine, although a cheaper version powered by the 700 cc version of the engine was available at launch.

Above: Expected competition from the Hillman Imp-powered Bond 875 three-wheeler led to Reliant purchasing Bond cars.

Opposite: The sporting Bond Equipe coupé was available through Triumph showrooms and Reliant hoped to replace it with versions of their own vehicles badged as Bonds.

Man Handled?
The Bond Equipe G.T.4S is built the way cars used to be.
By hand.

The reinforced glass fibre body is hand moulded.

The doors are hung by hand.

The car is assembled and trimmed by hand.

The various accessories are all fixed by hand.

Skin Deep ?
The Bond Equipe G.T.4S is a beautiful car.
Beautifully made. Beautiful to look at. And beautifully functional
The engine is the new 75 B.H.P. Triumph Mark III Spitfire giving the Equipe 12% increase in power
The chassis is all steel : The famous Triumph Herald " Double Backbone " chassis.
There is independent suspension on all four wheels.
There are waterproof, fade resistant, self adjusting, powerful disc brakes on the front wheels with increased caliper area.
There is a tiny 25' turning circle which is even tighter than a London taxi and which means it'll park virtually in its own length.

Colour Card
For a small extra charge you can have your Bond Equipe G.T.4S sprayed any colour you like.
Even tangerine.
But normally the car comes in
Winchester Blue
Signal Red
Prairie Beige
White
All very smart colours

The Body Beautiful
If you leave a conventional car outside all day and most nights, the rust gets it.

Rots the body.

Not so with the Bond Equipe G.T.4S

The glass fibre body can't rust. The steel doors and bulkhead are treated with a strong anti-corrosive.

Another thing.

The sort of minor accidents that dent steel body-work leave the Bond Equipe G.T.4S unmarked—glass fibre springs back to shape; you can touch up the paint yourself.

And if you do rip a hole, never fear, glass fibre can be built up again, then resprayed—at a fraction of the conventional repair cost.

Your Service
The Bond Equipe G.T.4S is built in association with Standard Triumph. A combination of Triumph Engineering and Bond Craftsmanship.

You get a hand built car.

And one that's backed up by the full servicing facilities of the country-wide Standard Triumph dealer network.

And one on which you get a 12,000 mile/12 month warranty.

The best of both worlds, in fact.

Internal Affairs?
The front bucket seats are unique to the Bond Equipe G.T.4S You sink into them, and they support your back and your shoulders and the backs of your legs as if they were just specially designed for humans. Which they were. Whichever of the 72 positions you care to adjust them to. The rear back seat is deep enough to loll in and is as deeply sprung as a club chair . . .

Interior trim is very smart.

Black seats. Deep grey carpet.

White roof trim. Polished walnut facia panel

Polished walnut window cappings

Polished wood steering wheel.

More to boot
Last, but not least, the Bond Equipe G.T.4S has a very large boot.

And a deep glove box.

And a wide parcel shelf (44"×12") above the back seat.

And a pair of deep pockets either side of the back seat.

AND THE CAR ITSELF WILL TAKE FOUR IN COMFORT
(including two man-sized men in the rear seat)

Price includes:
Fresh air heater
Demisters
Windscreen washers
Twin reversing lights
Safety harness anchor points
Vanity mirror
and, of course, full G.T. trim.

Built by Bond in association with Standard Triumph

The later Bond Equipe convertible based on the Triumph Vitesse. Replacement got as far as a design mock-up before plans came to an end.

Today many have gained the more powerful and widely available 850 cc engine, allowing the unexpected performance to surprise many a modern road user.

Uniquely wedge shaped, the Bond Bug had many components in common with the Robin range, all mounted under a wedge-shaped body inspired by an aeroplane cockpit and styled by Reliant regular designer Tom Karen. He would describe the Bond Bug as being aimed at drivers aged between seventeen and twenty-four who wanted but could not always afford a sports car. It featured a lift-up canopy rather than conventional doors.

This canopy could be removed completely to create a very drafty sporting convertible, and for the very nimble canvas side screens could be fitted in place of the side windows to allow access by sliding in from the side of the vehicle. (It was easy for the Dukes of Hazzard with a huge Dodge Charger, but less easy through the tiny aperture the Bond Bug offered.)

The Bond Bug remained in production until 1974 when Reliant discontinued it to allow the space its production occupied to be turned over to producing the phenomenally successful Reliant Robin. The first 500 Bugs were produced at the old Bond factory in Preston, thereafter production moving to the Reliant factory.

In 1994 a four-wheeled version of the Bond Bug was proposed by struggling Reliant that was seen on the television show *Trouble at the Top*. The chassis was a hybrid of Reliant Kitten front suspension and the rear suspension of the original Bond Bug. With a working title of Reliant Sprint, it would continue to be developed until 1998, by which time it was being described as the Reliant Clubman. By now the 850 cc engine had been fitted with fuel injection and a catalytic converter to meet modern emissions requirements. Both a coupé and a convertible made it as far as the prototype stage but never reached production.

The rights to the Bond Bug were sold on to Michael and Garry Webster, who developed it into the four-wheeled 'Webster bug' kit using a pre-1976 Mini rubber cone suspension

The Bond Bug was based on Reliant three-wheeled range running gear but retained the sporting Bond image.

subframe at the front and the mechanics from a Reliant Robin or Kitten. Twenty-three kits found homes before the company closed in the 1990s, along with a handful of recreation three-wheelers.

The first white Webster bug still exists in the hands of Garry Webster, proudly bearing the signature of styling wizard Tom Karen.

A Bond Bug three-wheeled chassis would find another unexpected claim to fame as the underpinnings of Luke Skywalker's land speeder in the 1977 film *Star Wars*, another vehicle in which Tom Karen would find himself involved in the styling.

Following the demise of Reliant the Bond Bug has a new lease of life as the four-wheeled Webster Bug kit.

10

Scimitar SS1 and Sabre

Seeing what they hoped was a gap in the marketplace following the demise of classic British sports cars such as the Triumph Spitfire and MG Midget, Reliant created the SS1 sports car.

The SS1 (standing for Small Sports model 1) plan started life as a sports body on the Reliant Kitten chassis with a tuned engine. This smaller sports design created by Tony Stevens got as far as gaining the name Cipher and the production of a prototype. Changes of management and ideas led to the car growing into a more conventionally sized sports car.

The SS1 was launched at the British International Motor Show in 1984 with an announced capacity to produce around 2,000 examples every year.

The Motor Show launch SS1 which would be much developed by the time it reached the showroom. A windscreen sticker clearly proclaimed that the colour scheme was not a production option.

In a break from Reliant's traditions, the SS1 took the form of separate injection moulded plastic panels made from a range of plastic types bolted to a separate backbone chassis unit. (It would be galvanised from 1986 for rust protection after the first 700 or so had been produced. Enthusiasts will tell you that the fitting of a single windscreen wiper at the same time is a handy way of telling if rust is likely to lurk beneath today.)

Vulnerable panels such as the bumpers and front wings were moulded from a special deformable reaction reinforced injection moulded plastic (often referred to as 'rubberised') which would flex rather than break in the event of an impact, and were fitted 'bolt on' style for easy removal and replacement rather than being bonded in place.

The chassis was a semi spaceframe with a central 'backbone' section of pressed members that surrounded the gearbox and led back to the rear-mounted differential. It included a series of tubular extensions to provide door frames and attachment points for the bolt-on front and rear wings. This design was allegedly chosen as it allowed for easier panel replacement in the event of an accident.

The downside of this style of design was that despite the majority of the panels being manufactured by Dunlop, when assembled there were often uneven panel gaps. Some unkind reviewers referred to the SS1 resembling a Lego kit.

The cause was that as some of the panels were formed from slightly different plastic materials, they all suffered from different shrinkage rates on cooling/hardening, which led to the potential uneven panel gaps, not all of which could be finessed away on the

The Ford CVH engine installed in the Motor Show launch car with the traditionally placed Reliant spare wheel.

final assembly line. Where the gaps could be fitted away the work took time and slowed down the production line, increasing the effective production cost of each vehicle. Some sources quoted a figure of 2.5 bonnets being manufactured for each SS1 produced due to these issues of variable production quality of the panels. Why Reliant took this route for body production when they had such a long and successful history of producing their own quality bodies in fibreglass has never been satisfactorily explained.

The Reliant-designed independent front suspension was a sophisticated design incorporating Vauxhall Chevette lower wishbones working with Reliant's own design of upper wishbones. Coil springs and horizontal shock absorbers were mounted on the front chassis cross member to save vertical space and allow for the low nose styling. At the rear there was an independent suspension system of fabricated semi-trailing arms with coil spring dampers.

Anti-roll bars front and rear completed the arrangement. The braking system came courtesy of the Austin Metro with discs at the front with drums at the rear.

In another break from their established tradition of producing as much of their vehicles in-house as possible the chassis were produced by Thyssen Nothelfer of Bielefeld, North Rhine-Westphalia in Germany. There has been much speculation over the years as to why Reliant took this step when it is considered that there was plentiful capacity at the Reliant factory to produce it themselves. The complexity of the design has been cited as a reason but this seems strange considering their proven ability previously to produce the chassis for their Scimitar and small four-wheeled vehicles.

The near horizontally mounted front shock absorbers are clearly visible here.

Thyssen Nothelfer retained some of the intellectual property rights to the advanced design, with Reliant owning 46 per cent at the start of production, rising to 60 per cent later. This chassis gave an almost perfect 50/50 weight distribution and massively contributed to the excellent handling of all versions of the SS1 family.

The SS1 was to be the last vehicle styled by Giovanni Michelotti, although he died before production began. Sadly he passed away before the final touches were put to the design but what Reliant already had was used.

With a nod to the UK market and weather conditions, a handsome angular hardtop with a heated rear window was available as an optional extra.

The 1.3-/1.4-litre models came as standard with steel wheels while the 1.6 would be supplied with alloy wheels. The 1.6 would also add tinted glass and velour upholstery to the package.

The Michelotti styling was controversial but fashionably up to date. At the front there were pop-up headlights as seen on the then recently discontinued Triumph TR7 (the Triumph TR7 parts bin would provide the pop-up motors for the headlights, while the Austin Metro would provide the light units, as it did for other small Reliants of the time) and seen elsewhere in such expensive cars as the current Porsche 928. The Ford Capri parts bin would provide the SS1 with wing mirrors and, when inverted, rear lights.

Legend has it that the styling Michelotti submitted for the SS1 had originally been turned down by his long-time client Triumph as a replacement for their long-running Triumph Spitfire small sports car.

Turbo technics answered observations regarding the lack of SS1 performance by developing a turbo kit with Rooster turbos.

The rear of the SS1 had a reasonably sized boot for a sports car, with an advertised capacity of 6.7 cubic feet. The boot also offered a small but handy lidded compartment under the boot floor for security or to keep tools and the like separate from the luggage.

Much space was liberated by the Reliant fashion of the time for mounting the spare wheel under the bonnet (a full-sized wheel on early vehicles, a space saver on later examples) as was also seen in the larger Scimitar. Reliant claimed this as a way of increasing safety in accidents in their brochures. The rear styling was classically simple but was described as 'curiously bland' by one report of the time.

The dashboard instrument cluster, steering column switches and interior buttons came from the Austin Metro range. The Triumph TR7 provided the basic seat frames, which could optionally be specified trimmed in leather.

As the Reliant engine was too small at 850 cc to power the SS1 and not able to be developed to a suitable larger capacity, Reliant sought a proprietary engine for power source. After considering units from British Leyland, Vauxhall, FIAT and Toyota, Reliant turned to long-standing partners Ford as they were already using their Ford V6 Cologne engine in the Scimitar GTE and GTC.

Under the bonnet Reliant adopted the new Bridgend-built Ford CVH overhead camshaft four-cylinder engine that was being used in many of Ford's smaller cars. This was mated to the rear-wheel-drive gearboxes from the Ford Sierra as drive was to the rear wheels rather than to the front as in the Fords that the engine was usually fitted to. Initially available in 1.3- and 1.6-litre capacities, a 1.4-litre version replaced the smaller engine when production of it ceased.

The SS1 front showing the fully developed headlights very different from the Motor Show car. Design touches such as the sculpted wheel arches were loved and loathed in turn by reviewers.

The smaller engine produced 69 horsepower in 1.3-litre form and 75 horsepower in the later 1.4-litre size. The 1.4-litre engine produced a top speed of 100 miles per hour and a 0–60 time of 12.7 seconds delivered through a four-speed gearbox.

The carburettored 1.6-litre engine that had seen service at Ford in the Fiesta XR2 and Escort XR3 offered more spritely performance from 95 horsepower. The larger engine pushed the top speed to 110 miles per hour and reduced the 0–60 time to 9.6 seconds driving through a standard five-speed gearbox.

The Reliant SS1 would have a moment of fame in the 1986 music video of the Pretenders song 'Don't Get Me Wrong' in which lead singer Chrissy Hynde would drive one in a video homage to the 1960s *Avengers* television show. Video trickery would even allow her to meet a 1960s version of Patrick Macnee. The car, registered C691 GOH, still exists.

When *Motor* magazine tested the SS1 1.6 they only managed a 0–60 time of 10.5 seconds and a top speed of 105 miles per hour but kindly attributed this to the fact the engine was of a low mileage and might be considered 'still tight'. They also speculated that the SS1 would have benefited from the adoption of the fuel-injected version of the CVH engine as used in the Escort XR3i, even if it required some redesign work to the interior to make room for parts of the injection system.

The performance from the early Ford engines was adequate and the handling excellent, if not especially refined, but alongside some of the competition the SS1 clearly lacked performance.

After-market tuners Turbo Technics would add a Rooster turbos turbocharger to the well-known Ford engine and produce a claimed 140 horsepower from it to create, according to their press releases, a 120 miles per hour car.

Reliant's response to the accusations of poor performance in the motoring press came in 1986 when a version powered by an 1800 cc CA18ET Nissan Turbocharged engine was announced. Christened the 1800Ti, it offered a huge jump in the performance figures over even the larger Ford engine. The power output from the new engine was 135 horsepower at 5,000 rpm.

The new engine transformed the performance of the SS1, raising the top speed to 126 miles per hour and giving a 0–60 time of 7.6 seconds. According to the Reliant brochure the new Nissan-powered 1800 Ti offered performance 'made for Autobahn driving'.

The launch handout brochure would sport a very prominent 'Powered by Nissan' flash on the front cover, something that must not have gone down well with Ford after supplying Reliant with engines for so many years.

The new Turbo model came with 14-inch alloy wheels and a new body-coloured boot lid spoiler as standard to differentiate them from the lesser models. For driver comfort there were now electric windows and alcantra trim.

General Motors looked at the small Reliant and wondered whether there was a market for the car in America. They were sufficiently interested to fund a 3-litre V6-engined prototype that became known as the SS2.

The styling was revised by famous British designer William Towns. Starting his design life in the Rootes group, Towns would go on to have a hand in the controversial Aston Martin Lagonda of the 1980s and numerous other small-production vehicles.

When the SS2 failed to make it into production the restyling work William Towns had carried out was used to facelift the UK production model in 1990 to create the Reliant SST

Above: As with many Reliant products, the parts bins of the Rover group provided the dashboard.

Below: The production answer to the Ford CVH engine's perceived lack of power was the installation of the 1,800 cc Nissan Turbocharged engine.

(the T standing for Towns after his design work, and brochures spoke of the vehicle being designed by him).

To answer criticisms in the press and from customers regarding poor panel fit on the SS1 the whole bodyshell was revised. Reliant reverted to their time-honoured system of producing the whole body in-house using fibreglass.

The restyled bodyshell was now formed from only two large sections forming the front and rear of the bodyshell. These two sections were bonded together on a jig in the usual Reliant manner together rather than the many bolt-on panels there had been previously. This both massively improved the finish of the vehicle as well as reducing the time it took to assemble them. Many of the panel lines that made the original look fussy from some angles were removed, with only the bonnet and boot lid common to the earlier versions.

The engines of the SST remained the basic 1.4-litre Ford CVH and the 1,800 cc Nissan Turbo unit.

For 1992 the SST was revised yet again to create the final version that would last until production ended in 1995. To distance the new model from the early SS1/SST models Reliant resurrected a name from their history and christened the new version the Sabre.

When the Nissan engine failed to meet the new UK emissions requirements and to simplify supply and spares in 1994 it was announced that both the Nissan and Ford engines were to be replaced by the technically more advanced aluminium twin overhead camshaft Rover K and T series engines. The 1.4-litre K series offered, according to the Reliant launch brochure, a top speed of 120 miles per hour and a 0–60 time of 8.5 seconds while the 2-litre T series engine offered a top speed of 'in excess' of 135 miles per hour and a 0–60 time of 6.5 seconds.

While there were examples of both at the Motor Show launch, only the K series engine reached production.

A very light and highly efficient design, the Rover K series engine would sadly go on to gain a malign reputation for failing head gaskets that would dog it for life and could be entirely blamed on poor maintenance.

The different materials and shrinkage rates used in adjoining components led to some large panel gaps.

The restyled Sabre did away with many of the eccentric styling cues of the earlier SS1 to create of more harmonious design with covered headlights.

Putting the power on the road were new OZ Premier 15-inch alloy wheels which became a standard fitment with larger 195/50 15 Bridgestone Expedia unidirectional tyres to help tame the power. Outside the bodyshell gained new flared wheel arches, side skirts and a fresh rear spoiler but otherwise remained largely unchanged. At the back Ford Transit rear lights would replace the Ford Capri ones used earlier.

This facelift neatly modernised the look of the car at minimal cost to Reliant, although some reviews commented that the final result looked 'fussy'.

For driver comfort there were electric windows and mirrors, a self-raising/retracting radio aerial, leather upholstery and a sophisticated for the day quartz coded radio cassette player as standard.

Sales Director Stewart Halstead described the Rover-engined Scimitar Sabres thus: 'The Scimitar is the sensible alternative. A unique combination of practicality, race bred road holding and performance, brilliant economy and fun to drive too.'

Production of the Reliant Scimitar/Sabre ended in 1995. Despite claims of a production capacity available of 2,000 cars per year at launch, total production of the SS1/SST/Sabre series of sports cars was around 2,200 examples.

Long after production of the SS1 series had ended and Reliant was no more the Rover special projects group used an SS1 chassis to produce a rear-engined V8 prototype that sadly never reached production.

The original SS1 and later Sabre.

Right: The rear of the SS1 and Sabre together. Note differing spoilers and Ford tail lights from different models.

Below: All models could be specified with a handsome hardtop, which came with a heated rear screen as standard.

11

The Last Days of Reliant

At the 1980 British Motor Show Tony Stevens displayed a Reliant Kitten-based sports car called the Cipher that was claimed to be capable of 94 miles per hour yet still return a healthy 44 miles per gallon. Stevens knew the vehicle needed considerable investment before it was production ready and gave Reliant the rights to produce two further prototypes before they lost interest. Internally they cited that they felt the 850 cc engine was insufficient to produce the performance they felt the vehicle required. Two examples still exist.

In 1980 Tony Stevens displayed the Reliant Kitten-based Cipher in which Reliant took an interest. It never reached production but the prototypes still exist. (Picture courtesy of Steve Poole)

The 1980s were difficult times for Reliant. Prices of four-wheeled cars from larger manufacturers had fallen and easy HP terms were now available to purchase them. Reliant were losing their dedicated and largely budget-conscious followers and sales were falling.

A much-publicised safety fault in their popular Reliant Robin range in 1979 led to the recall of around 25,000 for modification to the steering system. This cost the already struggling company a large amount of money and lost much goodwill amongst their customers.

Reliant called in the receivers in October 1990 and their assets were sold to Bean Industries, themselves once prolific motor manufacturers, for around £1.5 million. Bean Industries in turn called in the receivers in 1994. From this Reliant was acquired by the Avonex group in January 1995, who in turn had to call in the receivers in December 1995.

The remains of Reliant were purchased from the receivers by a consortium of businesses led by Jonathan Heynes in April 1996. Vehicle production began again by August 1996 with the famous Reliant Robin three-wheeler still finding a market among loyalist owners. Under the new owners production moved to a new, purpose-built factory in Burntwood, Staffordshire, in 1999.

In 2001 Reliant ceased production of their long-running and iconic three-wheeled vehicle range (the sporting Scimitar GTE had already departed to another manufacturer as detailed previously) to concentrate on the importation of the Italian three-wheeled Paigio Ape commercial vehicle (which could once again be driven on a motorcycle licence) and the French Ligier microcars. Poor sales and mounting debts would cause the doors to finally close in 2002.

In 2001 the Reliant range was replaced by imported versions of the Piaggio Ape, which could also be driven on a motorcycle licence.

The famous three-wheeled Robin would briefly live on in the hands of a company called B&N Plastics from 2001 but a number of legal and licensing issues led to production being halted later in 2002 and the name Reliant would not be seen on another vehicle.

The factory buildings have all now been demolished and replaced by a housing estate called Scimitar Park, whose road names commemorate the names of Reliant models Robin, Regal and Fox among others, all coming off a Tom Williams Way.

The Reliant Kitten/Fox engine and chassis would go on to form the running gear of the Tempest 850 sports car. Designed by TVR 350 designer John Box and kit car designer Ian Foster, the pedestrian body of the Kitten/Fox was replaced with an alloy-panelled sports body with fibreglass wings and nose.

The result was a sporting open car light enough to offer spritely performance and give a good account of itself in off-road trials events. The project would pass through several hands before ending up being manufactured by Reliant Spares in Worcestershire.

Initially designed in the days when kits of parts could be purchased to build your own Kitten from Reliant themselves, today they remain available to give a new lease of life to anyone with a time-worn Reliant Kitten or Fox looking for a new lease of life.

Over the sixty-five years of vehicle production Reliant could boast of having manufactured over two million vehicles and marketed them in one form or another in nine countries.

Once the Rootes group slipped out of UK ownership (American Chrysler had taken a controlling stake in 1967) Reliant would become the second largest UK-owned car manufacturer behind what would eventually become known as British Leyland, a position they would maintain until they closed down.

The Reliant Kitten would form the basis of the Tempest kit car. (Picture courtesy of Reliant Spares, Worcestershire)